What is God Like?

What is God Like?

Reflections on the Attributes of God

By Len Carlson
With Lloyd Mattson

River City Press
Minneapolis, Minnesota

ISBN: 09764232-7-8

Edited by: Lloyd Mattson, The Wordshed

Published by River City Press
http://www.rivercitypress.net
publisher@rivercitypress.net
4301 Emerson Avenue N.
Minneapolis, MN 55412

Printed in the USA by
Arrow Printing
Bemidji, Minnesota

Dedication

First Edition:

To my parents, Ed and Marge Carlson, of Chicago, Illinois, who during table grace taught me my first two attributes of God, God is great and God is good, then modeled God's goodness and greatness in their lifestyle and service to God through His church.

Len Carlson
1998

Second Edition:

To Len Carlson, beloved shepherd of the flock.

Not long after completing this series of sermons, Pastor Len was stricken with cancer. After long months of treatment and endless prayer, the Lord took him home. In his final days Pastor Len said, "For 21 years I taught my people how to live. Now I will teach them how to die." This he did, and at his triumphant memorial service, more than fifty pastors and friends from many faiths filled the lovely church Len built to bid a temporary good-bye to this gracious man of God.

Lloyd Mattson
2005

CONTENTS

Foreword

HE WHO CUTS HIS OWN WOOD IS TWICE WARMED. So said an old sage. We know what he meant. The thoughts in this small book first warmed our hearts as Pastor Len Carlson preached them at Bayside Baptist Church. Then the thoughts warmed us again as we turned sermons into these pages.

The function of a Foreword is to explain why a book is important and why the author was the right person to write it. Usually the publisher chooses a person of note to write the Foreword to enhance the book's credibility.

The importance of the book needs no bolstering, for knowing what God is like has eternal consequences for every person on earth. As to the author's credentials, any member of the Bayside congregation will vouch for them. However, the writers of the Foreword are quite un-notable. They are a somewhat retired couple who have spent more than a half-century in ministry together, preaching, writing, editing, and publishing, among other things.

Early in 1997 our pastor, Len Carlson, began an extended sermon series on the attributes of God. The themes and texts were routine enough, but the sermons were far from routine. Pastor Len's insights, gentle spirit, and creative presentations made us look forward eagerly to each Sunday. We will not soon forget *Any Old Rock Will Do*!

One Sunday, well into the series, our Sunday dinner conversation turned to the possibility of extending the life of Pastor Len's sermons through a devotional book. We had the tools and experience to do that. We bounced the idea off Bayside friends, then off Pastor Len. With some reticence, he granted permission.

Converting even the best of sermons into print takes some doing. No page can capture the subtleties of the pulpit. How do you spell a tear, a smile, or the wonder of listener serendipity? But we set to work, seeking to preserve Pastor Len's thoughts, while tampering as little as possible with his words.

Some tampering was inevitable, else what would editors do? We adjusted the mode from ear to eye, juggled occasional words and paragraphs, and indulged occasional editor intrusion. We regret that the results don't do justice to the preaching, but sermon books always fall short.

The book was our idea, and producing it became a heartwarming adventure. You too will be warmed as you read. Spread the warmth! Share *What Is God Like?* with your friends, particularly those who do not yet know how great is our God.

Lloyd and Elsie Mattson
The Wordshed
Duluth, Minnesota
1998

Introduction

IN TWENTY YEARS as pastor of Bayside Baptist Church, this is my second attempt to set forth the attributes of God through a series of sermons. The subject alone is enough to declare that it can be only an attempt, never an accomplishment.

I approached the sermon series with mixed feelings. I was excited that I and the congregation would have another opportunity to visit these majestic themes. Yet I was saddened to know that when the last Amen had sounded, I would have fallen short. My sole promise to the congregation was that I would do the best I could with the knowledge I had. But try as I might, lofty as my descriptions might be, clearly as I might preach, I knew I could not adequately describe our awesome God.

We can learn more about God sitting quietly in His presence than by listening to the finest preaching. God is to be enjoyed, not explained.

Yet explain we must to a darkening world. Throughout the series I lived with this tension: God had invited me to know Him. He had made Himself available to be known through the Scriptures. But in the end, I could not fully know Him. Still, I found myself mysteriously drawn to *try* to grasp His greatness and put it into words.

As each period of study and meditation ended, I came away fatigued and frustrated. I could not capture in words the elusive picture that emerged in my thoughts. To regain some sense of security, I would recalculate my bowling average. That, at least, reached a logical conclusion, restoring a sense of control. Such is the tension a finite sinner must face when trying to explain our infinite, holy God.

How often I prayed that God would come near me, that He would reveal His glory. How greatly I longed to see His majesty. How proper, yet how vain, were my prayers and longings. Moses, Isaiah, and John on Patmos barely survived the very experience I sought! Fortunately, the Holy Spirit interceded on my behalf. I can imagine Him saying to the Father, "Now isn't that cute! Len Carlson doesn't have a clue about what he is asking, but let's give him as much as he can handle."

I have always taught that the fear of the Lord was respect for God. Now I wonder if the fear of the Lord doesn't express the terror we experience in those moments when our holy, all-powerful God draws us close to Himself.

If these thoughts from the heart of a finite sinner enlarge your vision of God, I will be most satisfied. If these pages deepen your faith and trust, I will be more than satisfied. Whatever the worth of this small book, reader and author alike can only bow in humility before the God of Heaven and thank Him for one more grain of knowledge from the endless shores of His majesty.

Len Carlson
Bayside Baptist Church
Superior, Wisconsin
1998

1

God's Attributes: Why Should I Know Them?

You are worthy, our Lord and God, to receive glory and honor and power, for you created all things, and by your will they were created and have their being.

Revelation 4:11

WHAT IS GOD LIKE? Both Sunday school children and learned theologians ask that question. But neither will ever find the full answer. God in His eternal essence is beyond knowing: "No one has ever seen God."[1]

However, God was pleased to reveal much about Himself to fallen mankind. "God, the One and Only, who is at the Father's side, has made Him known."[2] The mystery of the incarnation! It is proper, then, to respond to questions about the nature of God by pointing to Jesus.

A seeker asks, "What is God like?"

We reply, "Look to Jesus! He said, 'If you really knew me, you would know the Father...Anyone who has seen me has seen the Father.'"[3]

The seeker asks further: "How can I know that God will love and forgive me? I've done terrible things."

We answer, "Jesus often associated with people who had done terrible things, yet He loved and forgave them. You can count on God's forgiveness, for He is just like His Son." Jesus said, "Believe Me when I say that I am in the Father and the Father is in me."[4]

As the Living Word, Jesus reveals the Father to those who seek Him, but there is another source of information about God: the written Word. Throughout these studies we will search the Scriptures to isolate specific characteristics—*attributes*—that are eternally present in God's person.

We will not explore all God's attributes by any means, but we will identify the major ones to answer the timeless question children and theologians ask, "What is God like?"

An *attribute* is a characteristic God has revealed as being true of Himself. When I say *God,* what comes to your mind? Love, perhaps; or grace, mercy, or strength. These are familiar attributes of God, but there are many more, and the value of knowing them is beyond imagining.

Our search will not be easy, for every attempt to describe God must fall short, as we note in the prophet Ezekiel's remarkable vision:

"High above on the throne was a figure like that of a man. I saw from what appeared to be His waist up He looked like glowing metal, as if full of fire, and that from there down He looked like fire; and brilliant light surrounded Him. Like the appearance of a rainbow in the clouds on a rainy day, so was the radiance around Him."[5]

The figure Ezekiel saw: was it a man as we would know one? No, but a figure "*like* a man." Did Ezekiel see a real waistline? No, he saw what "*appeared* to be His waist."

Ezekiel reported what "*looked* like glowing metal," and a radiance that had "the *appearance* of a rainbow in the clouds on a rainy day."

Like, likeness, appearance: what the prophet observed was greater than any words he could muster. He came close yet fell far short of describing his vision of God perfectly.

I acknowledge the same problem as I seek to present God's attributes. I will do my best, all the while knowing that my most carefully selected words must fail. Yet, for our spiritual growth, I must try.

There is another challenge: We will be treading deep water, and I must avoid becoming theologically academic and boring. All teaching about God must relate to life's everyday joys and struggles, or God will remain impersonal, distant. When I say, "*God is...*" then name an attribute, you have a right to say, "So what? Why should I care?"

We will build this introductory discussion around three statements that declare why Christians should care about the attributes of God.

KNOWING THE DIVINE ATTRIBUTES GUARDS AGAINST A LOW VIEW OF GOD

A hundred spiritual sicknesses can be traced to a low view of God. If life grows dull and worship becomes mechanical and boring, it is because we have lost sight of God's majesty. Psalm 73 tells about a faith that almost died. The psalmist began to envy the wicked he saw around him. They had more money than he, and less sickness. They led care-free lives; their kids did better in school. But there came a turning point: "When I tried to understand all this, it was oppressive to me till I entered the sanctuary of God, then I understood." [6]

What happened in the sanctuary? God came back into focus, and the depressed psalmist recovered from a temporary low view of God.

All manner of ills attend a low view of God. If you don't know that God is self-sufficient, you may think He needs your help and become a workaholic, filled with pride about how much the Lord depends on you. If you don't understand God's sovereignty, you may worry that the world is spinning out of control.

If you don't know that it is God who sets kings and presidents in authority, you may worry about politics. If you don't understand that God never changes, you may conclude that the Ten Commandments are only ten suggestions.

Failure to recognize God as all-powerful may tempt you to tackle tough problems by yourself. If you don't see God as all-knowing, you may squander prayer time telling Him what to do. If God is not your measure of true holiness, any moral code will do.

Those who are ignorant of God's grace and mercy often struggle to earn His favor on the premise that they can actually merit salvation. Ignorance of God's love leads to fear. Ignorance of God's wrath against all sin may lead you to think you are not accountable to Him for your life.

Spiritual sickness in all its forms can be traced to a low view of God, and that is why a grasp of God's attributes is so vital. Our faith will not grow beyond our perception of God; our churches can never rise higher than the view its people hold of God. A nation will never be greater than the vision its citizens possess of God's majesty.

Somehow, our souls and institutions are shaped by the image of God we hold in our hearts. A low view of God leads inevitably to a downward spiral that ends in idolatry, where something—often self—takes God's place. Knowing the full majesty of our eternal God protects us against deadly spiritual diseases

KNOWING GOD'S ATTRIBUTES ADDRESSES SPIRITUALITY QUESTIONS OF OUR DAY

The word *spirituality* no longer brings to mind hooded monks in a remote monastery or holier-than-thou folks we don't care to be among. Today, spirituality may mean horoscopes, psychics, relaxation techniques, yoga, transcendental meditation, angels, good-luck crystals, even Earth Day rallies.

Bizarre views of God are associated with spirituality. In fact, a person can be *spiritual* and not even believe there is a God! In the face of this confusion, Christians need to know what God has revealed about Himself. We know that God is light, but we must also know that God is unchanging: He cannot deny or contradict Himself.

Are all mystical experiences involving light genuine encounters with God? Certainly not. Satan can disguise himself as an angel of light. Does light in a near-death experience prove God's presence? Not when the experience leads to convictions contrary to the Bible.

KNOWING GOD'S ATTRIBUTES HELPS US YIELD CONTROL OF OUR LIVES

Our sinful nature tries to reduce God to manageable terms, to use Him for our own ends. The health/wealth gospel—which fortunately seems to be fading—teaches people to claim Bible verses that deal with prosperity, then find two or three friends to agree with them in prayer. That, they say, obligates God to supply what the person claims. They have God right where they want Him.

We long to control God, but story after story in the Bible teaches submission and humility as the only source of spiritual security.

Which of these churches do you think has the greater potential for ministry? The first church: "We've got a problem. We're not sure how to solve it, but we've got our best people trying to come up with an answer. Frankly, we're worried." The second church: "We've got a problem we can't seem to solve, but we're not worried. This isn't our church anyway, it's the Lord's. We keep looking to God for direction, and we expect soon to discover what He wants us to do."

Think of that glorious day when we catch our first glimpse of God in all His glory. Our first thought will surely be, God is so incredible! Why did I struggle so long to be in control? Why didn't I just let go and trust Him?

Why should we care to know God's attributes? So that we will cease trying to manipulate God, worry less, surrender fully to Him, and live in peace and security.

1. John 1:18
2. John 1:18
3. John 14:7, 9
4. John 14:11
5. Ezekiel 1:26-28
6. Psalm 73:16-17

2

Any Old Rock Will Do

Our Self-existent, Self-sufficient God

The God who made the world and everything in it is the Lord of heaven and earth and does not live in temples build by hands. And He is not served by human hands, as if He needed anything, because He Himself gives all men life and breath and everything else.   Acts 17:24-25

WE BEGAN OUR STUDY of God's attributes with this question: What is God like? The question is important because proliferating cults and the growing public interest in the supernatural have created an abundance of misrepresentations concerning the nature and character of God. In this chapter we will consider two of God's attributes: *self-existence* and *self-sufficiency.*

Imagine a mother driving her daughter to school:

"Mommy, who made the trees and grass and flowers?"

"God made them, dear."

"Who made us?"

"Well, God made us also."

"Then, who made God?"

Maybe you have been that mommy—or daddy, grandma, grandpa, aunt or uncle. Who made God? You know the answer, but you also know that your young passenger will never understand it, because you don't understand it. You give the only possible answer: No one made God; He always existed.

We long to answer children's questions to enjoy the look of understanding on their faces, but as our answer to Who made God? rolls around in little heads, we see more frustration than satisfaction. You can almost hear the child's thoughts: *Someone had to make God!*

OUR SELF-EXISTING GOD

Everything we know has a beginning and end, everything from aspirin to computers, so we can't imagine anyone or anything that always existed. Yet there never was a time when God did not exist and there never will be a time when God ceases to exist. He owes His origin and continuing existence to no one.

The writer of Genesis assumed God's existence before time: "In the beginning God created..."[1] When there was no heaven to display His glory, no people He could love, no angels to sing His praises, no Satan to oppose His purposes, God was there, with only Himself for company—Father, Son and Holy Spirit.

When Moses asked God His name, He replied, "I AM WHO I AM."[2] When certain Jews challenged Jesus He replied, "Before Abraham was born, I am."[3] On another occasion He said, "For as the Father has life in Himself, so

He has granted the Son to have life in Himself."[4] John wrote concerning Jesus, "In Him was life."[5]

God has life without beginning or end. He is the source of all life, from the single-cell amoebae to the most complex organism. God gives all things life—a part of His very nature. Nothing could come alive by itself, and only the life-giving God can restore life to the dead—our blessed hope!

Our lungs breathe and our hearts beat apart from thought or conscious command—a gift from Creator God in whom we "live and move and have our being."[6] Our will to live is very strong, but our ability to live can become fragile. Every moment of life is God's gift, and He has the right to hold us to account.

Some New Age teachings would lead us to believe that with sufficient enlightenment a person can achieve a god-like level. This low view of deity is at best absurd, at worst, blasphemous. To think that we who know our beginning and end, who get sick and need medicine, who grow tired and cranky could become like God is utterly ridiculous. Our self-existent God stands alone in eternity. Settle for nothing less!

OUR SELF-SUFFICIENT GOD

Of all the thoughts in these discussions, God's self-sufficiency is perhaps the most difficult to accept, not because biblical support is lacking, but because pride rebels. Two fears arose in my heart as I wrestled with this truth: First, I feared you wouldn't understand because I would fail to explain God's self-sufficiency well enough. I apologize in advance for that. Second, though you might understand the truth, you wouldn't like it, for the concept batters the ego.

This theme is not popular in a society preoccupied with self-esteem. If God has no needs, then He can be no more satisfied because we serve Him or less satisfied when we refuse to serve Him. He depends on us for nothing. To suggest that God has needs would suggest an imperfection.

Need is a creature word. It cannot apply to the Creator. We have needs, but God can have no needs, certainly no needs mere humans could fill. God did not create the universe because He was bored, nor did He create people because He was lonely. Our self-sufficient God is entire, lacking nothing, fully content in His eternal being.

Now I must speak with great care: A life of devotion, praise, and purity cannot enhance God's stature any more than the atheist's blasphemous life can lessen God's stature. God does not need us to be satisfied. If He did, then God would be dependent on us to fulfill a need. God's relationship to His creation is voluntary, not of necessity. Nothing we can do obligates God to act on our behalf.

Perfect attendance in church for a year does not obligate God to improve our lot in life. Every benefit we enjoy flows from His good pleasure, not from constraint. Not so with us. Should you invite me and my wife to dinner every Friday for a year, I would feel constrained to return the favor, for your kindness met a real, personal need. But God has no needs, therefore He can never incur debt.

A subtle drive moves Christians to think, "If I do good things for God, surely He will do good things for me." We bargain with God! But Job went to church every morning to sacrifice for His family, yet He lost everything. How did Job respond? "The Lord gave and the Lord has taken away; may the name of the Lord be praised."[7]

God relates to us only on the basis of grace—His good pleasure. "He chose us in Him before the creation of the world to be holy and blameless in His sight. In love He predestined us to be adopted as His sons through Jesus Christ....and He made known to us the mystery of His will *according to His good pleasure.*"[8] God Honors our devotion, not because we earn His honor, but because He is pleased to honor us.

By now you may be feeling that God is cold and impersonal. Be patient! We are considering here but one of God's many attributes: self-sufficiency. The warm fuzzies—Love, Grace, Goodness—are yet to come.

We conclude, then, that God is all powerful, everywhere present, fully knowing, perfect; satisfied and sufficient in Himself, needing no help or helpers. As our text notes, God is not served by human hands, as though He needed anything.

But this leads to the hard question: If God does not need us, what is our role before Him?

ANY OLD ROCK WILL DO

Indeed, God does not *need* us, but He chooses to use us according to His good pleasure. It is crucial to distinguish between need and choice, lest we sin by thinking of ourselves more highly than we ought. Consider this rock. *[Pastor Len held aloft an oval-shaped rock, slightly smaller than a football].*

John the Baptist preached repentance to an audience that included Jews who were filled with religious pride. "Do not begin to say to yourselves, 'We have Abraham as our Father,' For I tell you that out of these stones God can raise up children for Abraham."[9]

On the day of Jesus' triumphal entry into Jerusalem, a crowd lined the road shouting praises. The Pharisees ordered Jesus to stop them, but He responded, "If they keep quiet, the stones will cry out."[10]

Does God want people to become His children to take up the work of His kingdom? Yes! But if every Christian refused, would God be less self-sufficient and long for some need to be fulfilled? If the thought ever crosses your mind that somehow God can't do without you, think again. Any old rock will do!

Does God want His people to gather together to worship His Son in church? Yes! But if no one obeyed, would God

23

be less self-sufficient, hungering for praise? God's resources are unlimited. Any old rock will do.

Does God want pastors to preach the gospel and care for His body, the church? Yes! But if every preacher failed, would God be less self-sufficient, less in stature, or suffer for want of leaders? No, because any old rock will do.

Though God does not *need* you, He longs that you come to faith and serve Him. But as you serve remember our text: God is not served by human hands, as though He needed anything. Service is a privilege God grants according to His good pleasure.

To guard against even the most fleeting thought that somehow God just can't do without you, remember this sound: *[Pastor Len dropped the rock with a startling* ***BOOM!]***

Any old rock will do.

1. Genesis 1:1
2. Exodus 3:14
3. John 8:58
4. John 5:26
5. John 1:4
6. Acts 17:28
7. Job 1:21
8. Ephesians 1:4, 5, 9
9. Luke 3:8
10. Luke 19:40

3

Ruler of Heaven and Earth
God's Sovereignty

Remember this, fix it in mind....I am God, and there is no other; I am God, and there is none like me....What I have said, that will I bring about; what I have planned, that will I do. Isaiah 46:8, 9, 11

His dominion is an eternal dominion, His kingdom endures from generation to generation....He does as He pleases with the powers of heaven and the peoples of the earth.
Daniel 4:34-35

THE WORD *SOVEREIGN* has to do with the authority to rule. We use it with kings as they govern nations and people. Sovereignty implies both the power to rule and dominion, a place to rule. God's sovereignty describes His supreme authority over people, over angelic beings, over nature, over all creation.

Of necessity, sovereignty involves other attributes of God. To be sovereign, He must be *omniscient,* all-knowing. Presidents know most of what their staff people are doing, but God knows all that has happened and all that will happen. Not the smallest bit of knowledge escapes Him. If there were something God did not know, He would not be sovereign.

To be sovereign, God must be *omnipotent,* all-powerful. If any force had one shred more power than God, He would not be sovereign. God's power exceeds the most terrible nuclear device. Not a particle of energy in the universe can stray beyond His control.

To be sovereign God must be *omnipresent,* everywhere present. There is no place or moment in time where God does not dwell in His fullness. Should one spot in the universe exist that was void of His presence, God would not control that spot and He would not be sovereign.

Finally, God must be *independent*, totally free of obligation to consult anyone. If someone could alter God's plan or influence His thought, He would not be independent and therefore not sovereign. The God we know stands unchallenged; the eternal, sovereign Ruler.

GOD'S SOVEREIGNTY AND THE BELIEVER
The knowledge of God's sovereignty brings mixed feelings to the Christian. We feel frustrated when God, who has the power to control every circumstance, fails to exercise that power as we think He should.

How often in the face of horrible evil or personal suffering have we heard, "God could have prevented this!" It is true; He could have, for God is sovereign. We walk out of a hospital, a funeral home, a failed marriage. Our home burns, our business fails. In frustration we cry, *"Why?"*

Yet, when we dare to bow before God's sovereign grace and cry out in faith, "I don't understand, but I will trust God to fulfill His purpose for my life," we gain a measure of comfort.

GOD'S SOVEREIGNTY IS ABSOLUTE

God rules from the highest position. An earthly ruler enjoys only limited authority. An enemy may overrun his country. A political foe unseat him. Inevitably, death will one day take him. Earthly sovereigns must always be limited, but God's reign is eternal, absolute.

God must be all-sovereign or He is not sovereign at all. The gods of mythology knew limitations and competitors, but the God of the Bible has no peers. Can you imagine Jehovah seeking permission to act? "Who has known the mind of the Lord? Or who has been His counselor? Who has ever given to God, that God should repay Him?"[1] To suggest a limit to divine authority leads to absurd questions. "This is what the Lord says, Israel's king and redeemer, the Lord Almighty, I am the first and I am the last: apart from me there is no God."[2]

The increasing proliferation of cults and false religions leads many to protest Christianity's claim that our God is sovereign. It is not politically correct to deny equal stature to other religious viewpoints. But if the Bible is true, then God's authority excludes compromise. There cannot be multiple sovereigns.

GOD'S SOVEREIGNTY OVER EVIL

Neither evil's mysterious entry or Adam and Eve's fall into sin caught God by surprise. Before He created the world, He foresaw the effects of evil on mankind and planned a remedy.[3] Yet evil, sometimes horrendous evil, continues to frustrate believers. How can a sovereign God allow evil to exist?

No satisfying explanation will ever be presented on earth, including mine, but we must never allow the fog of ignorance lead us to conclude that somehow evil will one day foil God's plans. If evil grew beyond God's control, He would no longer be sovereign.

History is moving toward the return of Christ and evil cannot delay that event, nor can faith hasten it. As with His first coming, Jesus' return will be in the fullness of time, at the moment God has determined. Evil will not influence God's timing.

In His sovereign pleasure God chose to create humans with the capacity to choose. We are free to disobey God for selfish purposes. Though God knew beforehand how humans would employ free will, evil in no way moved beyond His control. But could not God have prevented evil in the first place? Of course, but that would have robbed people of the capacity to make choices. The essence of evil is asserting self-will over God's will. God allows evil to exist within His authority to fulfill His loving purpose for mankind.

The Bible offers many pictures of the relationship between God, mankind, and Satan, the personification of evil. Nowhere is the picture more dramatic than in the story of Job. We are allowed to listen in on a conversation in Heaven as Satan seeks permission to afflict God's faithful servant Job. God grants permission, limited at first; then increasingly severe, stopping just short of taking Job's life. The story makes it clear who is supreme.

Jesus' words to Peter also reveal Satan's relationship to mankind: "Satan has asked to sift you as wheat. But I have prayed for you that your faith may not fail."[4] This assures us that Satan must gain permission to touch a follower of Christ.

The ultimate evil—killing God's Son—was not a triumph of Satan. "The reason my Father loves me is that I lay down my life—only to take it up again. No one takes it from me, but I lay it down of my own accord. I have authority to lay it down and authority to take it up again. This command I received from my Father."[5]

In His sovereign purpose, God sometimes uses evil to accomplish a greater good. Joseph said to his brothers, who years before had sold him into slavery, "You intended to harm me, but God intended it for good." [6] Paul spoke of a physical ailment as a thorn in the flesh, a messenger of Satan, but he declared the thorn drove him deeper into the arms of God. Physical weakness allowed God's strength to be displayed. [7]

Though evil persists, its power and scope are limited and temporary; confined within the bounds God sets. Satan's rebellion is not a contest between equals.

GOD'S SOVEREIGNTY: OUR SOURCE OF SECURITY

As we learn to accept by faith the unanswered questions evil raises, the assurance of God's sovereignty brings comfort and security. Inner peace does not come by demanding that God explain His action or lack of action. Great faith often is forged in the heat of confusion as evil runs rampant. Remember Job's response in the face of monstrous evil, "The Lord gave, and the Lord has taken away; may the name of the Lord be praised." [8]

God did not devise His eternal plan for our convenience, nor will He yield to our plea for explanations. Sovereignty is God's very character. It is His purpose, always, to lead us deeper into faith and trust. Of this we can be sure: God will fulfill every promise He ever made, and one day He will destroy practitioners of evil and reward all who have been made righteous through faith in His Son.

Meanwhile, in the moral and spiritual conflict that rages around us, we can rejoice in the certainty that all who belong to God are on the winning side; all who reject God's Son are on the losing side. "God exalted (Jesus) to the highest place and gave Him the name that is above every name, that at the name of Jesus every knee should bow...and every tongue confess that Jesus Christ is Lord, to the glory of God the Father." [9]

1. Romans 11:34-35
2. Isaiah 44:6
3. Revelation 13:8
4. Luke 22:31
5. John 10:17-18
6. Genesis 50:19-20
7. 2 Corinthians 12:7-10
8. Job 1:21
9. Philippians 2:9-11

4

Yesterday, Today, Forever
God's Immutability

In the beginning you laid the foundations of the earth, and the heavens are the work of your hands. They will perish, but you remain; they will all wear out like a garment. Like clothing you will change them and they will be discarded. But you remain the same, and your years will never end.

Psalm 102:25-27

WE LIVE IN A WORLD of constant change. In the days of Moses and Abraham, people lived in tents. Today we live in houses. They walked or rode animals; we favor cars, planes, and trains. To communicate, the ancients sent messengers on foot. We telephone, fax, e-mail, and occasionally lick stamps. They grew crops and tended flocks; we manufacture goods and sell services and information.

Do we have *anything* in common with biblical times? Indeed! We serve the same God; He has not changed. That is the bridge between our day and Bible times. What God expected of the ancients He expects today. His love for Moses and Abraham was no greater or less than His love for you and me.

Theologians speak of God's *immutability*—no mutation, no change. Created organisms mutate but God does not. Nothing greater than God exists that could cause Him to change. He offers Himself as the source of stability in our constantly changing world.

The best the Bible writers could do was to compare God with rock, which seemed not to change through the centuries. Today we know that over time even rocks wear away. God is more unchanging than mountains.

GOD'S CHARACTER DOES NOT CHANGE

"Before the mountains were born or you brought forth the earth and the world, from everlasting to everlasting you are God."[1] God, who had no origin and will never cease to be, is eternally the same. He exists in perfection; He cannot improve, and since He has no flaw He cannot change for the worse. God exists outside of time so He cannot age. He is no older today than He was when He talked with Moses.

God cannot grow smarter for He knows all things—there is nothing for Him to learn. God's mood never fluctuates, no highs or lows. He has no powers today He has not always had and He has never lost a power He once possessed. Existing in perfect wholeness, God cannot mature in character.

When Moses asked God for His name, God replied, "I AM WHO I AM."[2] He did not give Moses a name so much as a description of His unchanging being. From the burning bush God revealed His self-existence and eternal sameness. A glorious truth! What God was to Moses, He is to us—the great I Am.

God does not pursue holiness; He is holiness. He does not work at being more loving; God is love. God does not seek after truth; He is truth. God's character never changes, but not so with humans! Aging, failing health, or tragedy may cause people to become bitter. A patient person may grow angry; a positive person cynical, a caring person indifferent. But our God can never be less truthful, honest, holy, patient, or gracious than He always has been. When God disciplines us we may think He has changed, but God's acts are always motivated by love. He disciplines because He cares. He wants His children to grow in faith and holiness.

Many believe that the Old Testament God differs from the God of the New Testament. Not so! Though God's acts in individuals will differ according to their response to His eternal purpose, His character remains forever unchanged.

GOD'S TRUTH DOES NOT CHANGE

God's immutability has been attacked from outside the church and, sadly, from within as church leaders place higher value on being politically correct than biblically sound. They believe that the teachings of the Bible have fallen behind changing social and moral attitudes. They say that though the Bible may have served previous generations well, it does not fit our day. Sin and repentance are considered to be outdated.

The 60s and early 70s were pivotal years as young people rebelled against the establishment. *Situation Ethics,* a book written by a seminary professor, advanced the idea that absolute right and wrong cannot be determined; it is proper for anyone to do whatever seems most loving at the moment because love is the highest biblical value.

For example: A young wife and mother of three is in jail. It is suggested that if she submits to sex with a guard, she could be set free. What should she do? The Bible declares, Thou shalt not commit adultery. Situation ethics

33

says, For the good of her family, adultery would be the most loving thing to do. Not an easy decision, given the moral climate of our day! But Isaiah 40:8 declares, "The grass withers and the flowers fall, but the word of our God stands forever." If we believe that God cannot change, then we must believe that His Word does not change.

We change our minds, take back our words and often regret what we said. God never changes His mind, takes back one word, or regrets anything He said. New information may change our minds, but God never receives new information. To Him the past, present and future are one, hence He always speaks with eternal authority. His words are absolute.

GOD'S PURPOSES DO NOT CHANGE

"And He made known to us the mystery of His will according to His good pleasure, which He purposed in Christ, to be put into effect when the times will have reached their fulfillment—to bring all things in heaven and on earth together under one head, even Christ."[3]

God's long purpose is clear. These verses include the plan of salvation for today as well as God's ultimate plan to unite   all things in heaven and on earth under the headship of Christ. He will do that when the times He has allotted are fulfilled. History moves toward Christ's return, when God will complete His purpose for this phase of planet Earth.

How does God's long plan relate to your car accident, arthritis, lousy boss, or annoying neighbor? I don't know. But I do know that one day everything in heaven and on earth will fall under the Lordship of Jesus. In that day you will be deeply grateful that God privileged you to bear His name as you dealt with the accident, arthritis, lousy boss and annoying neighbor.

God lays plans with full knowledge of the past, present and future. He is never surprised, never experiences emergencies, and never overlooks a detail, no matter how small. What He has purposed in Christ includes you! You can yield to His plan or resist it, but the plan will move forward on schedule, neither slowed by your resistance nor hastened by your yielding. However, as you become a willing part of God's purpose, you will be enriched beyond anything you can imagine, not only in this life but through eternity.

God's long purpose or His present plan of salvation will never change. Salvation will always rest on repentance of sin, faith in Christ and a life of discipleship. The God we know declares, "I the Lord do not change."[4]

1. Psalm 90:2
2. Exodus 3:14
3. Ephesians 1:9-10
4. Malachi 3:6

Psalm 40:30 (Alus)

5

El-Shaddai
God's Omnipotence

When Abram was ninety-nine years old, the Lord appeared to Him and said, "I am God Almighty; walk before me and be blameless."   Genesis 17:1

I am the Alpha and the Omega, says the Lord God. "Who is, and who was, and who is to come, the Almighty."

Revelation 1:8

COULD GOD MAKE A ROCK so big He couldn't lift it? That question has been around for centuries. Today it is raised most often by junior-high kids trying to stump their Sunday school teacher. We'll let the question introduce the theme of this study: God's *omnipotence.*

Really, it is a non-question, like, Have you stopped beating your wife? No matter how you answer, you lose. If God *could* make a rock so big He couldn't lift it, there would be something He could not do and He would not be all-powerful. On the other hand, if God was unable to make a rock that big, He would still be wanting in total power. But we will leave trick questions for others to ponder and consider the meaning of the name God revealed to ninety-nine-year-old Abram: *El-Shaddai,* the Almighty, the God of all power.

Power appeals to almost everyone—generally to one's lower nature. Power promises control over circumstances and people. Power stirs pride and self-sufficiency. Christians who hunger for power need to check their motives.

Prayers for spiritual power are often tainted by a desire for the attention power draws. Power corrupts. Consider the recent track record of nationally-known, highly-gifted religious leaders. Christians easily forget that "the one who has been entrusted with much, much more will be asked."[1]

The United States President is called the most powerful man on earth, the leader of the Free World. Heady stuff! Yet presidential power shrinks to infinity when compared with the power of Jesus Christ, ruler of the kings of the earth.[2] The King of kings wields ultimate power. If an equal power existed, God would not be El-Shaddai, the Almighty.

God's power was not an acquired power, and it has never increased. Power belongs to Him because power is the nature of God. But having said that, let me startle you. *There are things God can't do!*

LIMITATIONS OF GOD'S POWER

You may think Carlson is starting to crack (and that may be open for discussion) but the statement is true: there are some things God just can't do.

God can do everything He chooses to do, but He is bound by the perfection of His character. God cannot die, or sin, or lie, or break a promise. God cannot cease loving you. God cannot deceive, trick, or tempt you. God always acts in harmony with His holy nature.

God's strength is affirmed in the things He cannot do. His perfection allows no weakness.

Our knowledge of God's nature assures us that He will never act in a capricious manner. He will always look to our best interests. Knowing this eases our hearts in difficult times. We know that God is never the author of distress or temptation. "When tempted, no one should say, 'God is tempting me.' For God cannot be tempted by evil, nor does He tempt anyone."[3] Yes, there are things God cannot do. He cannot act so as to deny His nature. Christian, Rejoice!

DEMONSTRATIONS OF GOD'S POWER

The evidence of God's unlimited power surrounds us. Arrogant mortals who reject God's Word ascribe power to Nature, but they never explain Nature's origin nor its evident order. The same mortals ascribe final authority to humanity, thereby denying accountability to God—if indeed they acknowledge that God exists. But the discerning mind cannot escape the evidence for God's existence and power.

The creation demonstrates God's power

"What may be known of God is plain to them. For since the creation of the world God's invisible qualities—his eternal power and divine nature—have been clearly seen, being understood from what has been made, so that men are without excuse."[4] God designed the human spirit to recognize His Godhead, power, and majesty in the creation. Mankind has no excuse for turning its back on the Creator.

The universe was created by God's power without pre-existing materials. "By faith we understand that the universe was formed at God's command, so that what is seen was not made out of what was visible."[5] "He is our father....the God who gives life to the dead and calls things that are not as though they were."[6]

God needed no raw material; His purpose and power enabled Him to bring into existence the universe with its infinitely complex systems. "And God said, 'Let there be light,' and there was light."[7]

Challenge any university research staff made up of the sharpest scientific minds to duplicate God's feat. Tell them to create anything they want, the only stipulation being that they start with nothing, a vacuum void of a single charged particle, atom, or molecule—total nothingness. They would pronounce the task impossible.

The universe is the most dramatic evidence of divine power that knows no limitations. We walk in the creation, swim in it, picnic in it, marvel at its delicate balance and beauty. And we stand in awe to know that God started it all with nothing. El Shaddai!

Miracles demonstrate God's power

Miracles of the Old Testament, New Testament, and present-day bear witness to an all-powerful God. The natural laws He created provided an orderly, predictable world. When He chooses, God may temporarily suspend natural law to work miracles.

Natural law decrees that objects heavier than water will sink. Yet in Elisha's day, God made an ax head float. And you recall that Jesus—and Peter—walked on water.

Natural law sets the time when reproductive systems cease to function, yet Abraham and Sarah were promised a son in their 90's. In response to Sarah's skepticism, God said to Abraham, "Is anything too hard for the Lord?"[8]

In the birth of His Son, God carried the miracle a step further: Jesus was conceived without a human father. The angel said to an astonished Mary, "Nothing is impossible with God."[9]

God works startling miracles. He caused the rain to cease for three years in Elijah's day. Jesus fed five thousand with five loaves and two small fish. He healed the sick and raised the dead. God who established natural law can suspend it when He so purposes. El Shaddai!

Redemption demonstrates God's power

We move now from what we can see to what can't be seen. You can't hold sin in your hand, weigh it, or put it in a bottle. Yet sin is still very real. You can feel sin and see its effects. You can sense sin with your mind and emotions. Sin is a spiritual concept, and we are spiritual as well as physical beings. Physical realities respond to physical forces. Spiritual realities must be dealt with by faith.

God calls all moral failure sin, and sin places us under God's judgment. But faith in Jesus Christ and His sacrificial death on the cross cancels the sin debt. God said that is so. He alone has the power to forgive sin's debt.

I can't forgive sin—I have no power or authority to do that. God reserves forgiveness to Himself. Only the blood of Jesus can cleanse from sin, for this was God's provision.

The power to forgive has eternal consequences. In the light of eternity, the spiritual world is more real and certainly more enduring than life on Earth. One day Earth life will cease, but no person will ever cease to be.

The soul is more real than the body. The body will return to dust, but our souls—our real being—will live forever. Redemption power, the power to cleanse us from sin, resides only in Almighty God. El Shaddai!

1. Luke 12:48
2. Revelation 1:5
3. James 1:13
4. Romans 1:19-20
5. Hebrews 11:3
6. Romans 4:17
7. Genesis 1:3
8. Genesis 18:14
9. Luke 1:37

6

The All-knowing One
God's Omniscience

O Lord, you have searched me and known me. You know when I sit and when I rise, you perceive my thoughts from afar. You perceive my going out and my lying down; you are familiar with all my ways. Before a word is on my tongue you know it completely, O Lord. Psalm 139:1-4

Who has understood the mind of the Lord, or instructed Him as His counselor? Whom did the Lord consult to enlighten Him, and who taught Him the right way? Who was it that taught Him knowledge or showed Him the path of understanding? Isaiah 40:13-14

BY WAY OF REVIEW: We understand that God had no origin—He always existed as He is today. God requires no help or helpers, as though He needed assistance. God has never changed. He holds supreme authority and power: God does as He pleases, limited only by His holy character. He cannot sin, lie, or forget a promise.

To this list we now add another attribute: God is all-knowing, *omniscient.* We acquire knowledge through study, observation, and experience. We are constantly learning, teaching and being taught. For us, knowledge accumulates, but this is not so with God. He has always known everything there is to know.

GOD'S OMNISCIENCE INCLUDES FULL SELF-KNOWLEDGE

God never experiences an unexpected moment, a time when He does not know what to do. We say, "I don't understand!" God has never said that. We say, "I don't know how I would react in that situation." God has never said that. We say, "I'll figure it out when I get there," or, "I never knew that about myself!" God always knows what He would do in every situation. He is never surprised; He never leaves anything to chance. Throughout eternity, God has never faced an uncertain moment.

God does not know some things better than others. He is not good at Math but poor at Geography. God never discovers anything; He is never startled or shocked. He never wonders, ask questions, looks up information, or changes His mind because of new data. You can't tell God a joke, for jokes depend on the unexpected.

God not only knows everything about Himself, He knows everything about everyone. He understands all natural laws. Science can only seek out what God already knows—nature's mysteries, causes and effects, human feelings and desires. God knows everything about space, time, life, death, good, and evil. The Creator God, source of all creation, is the master of all knowledge.

GOD'S OMNISCIENCE INCLUDES THE FUTURE

With God there is no past, present or future. At the dawn of creation He saw history from beginning to end and each of the billions who would inhabit Planet Earth throughout time.

God knows no future. What we call future is as certain to God as the past and present. "After this I will return and rebuild David's fallen tent. Its ruins I will rebuild, and I will restore it...says the Lord, who does these things that have been known for ages."[1] Across the course of time the Lord simply does what He has always known He would do.

Under the Holy Spirit's guidance, Old Testament prophets predicted events far in the future and we stand amazed to note their fulfillment. But from God's perspective, prophecy is simply the unfolding of history. The future is the same as the past and present in God's sight. Nothing ever catches Him by surprise, and nothing He foresees ever fails.

GOD'S OMNISCIENCE INCLUDES US

God knows the number of hairs on our heads, our genetic make-up, and our every thought—good or bad. Nothing remains hidden from God. Our prayers do not provide new information. "Before they call I will answer; while they are still speaking I will hear."[2]

God's omniscience brings both comfort and wonder. It is good to know that nothing can happen that God did not see beforehand, and equally good to know that He is preparing us today for experiences yet to come; the difficult times as well as greater opportunities for service in His kingdom.

But if we could strip God of one attribute, we might choose omniscience. An awareness of His full knowledge can be unsettling, for it includes our deepest secrets. "You have set our iniquities before you, our secret sins in the light of your presence."[3]

No one on earth saw Cain murder his brother Abel, but God saw. "Where is your brother?" He asked.

When Sarah heard she would bear a child in her old age, she tried to hide her laughter, but the Lord saw. "Why did you laugh?" He asked.

David tried to conceal his sin with Bathsheba, but God saw. He sent the prophet Nathan to say, "You are the man!"

"You perceive my thoughts from afar. Before a word is on my tongue you know it completely, O Lord."[4] "This is what the Lord says: This is what you are saying...but I know what is going through your mind."[5]

God knows all our thoughts all the time. He knows our heart thoughts as we worship, sing, pray and meditate on His goodness and grace. And He knows our evil thoughts. God's perfect knowledge would be deeply troubling if we did not know His unconditional love.

How good to know that sinful thoughts do not drive away God's love. He brings secret sins to light so that the sinner will seek forgiveness. "Search me, O God, and know my heart; test me and know my anxious thoughts. See if there is any offensive way in me, and lead me in the way everlasting."[6]

We can be sure God's search will be thorough. Nothing remains hidden from His eyes. Yet we need not fear, for what greater security could there be than to know that God still loves us, even though He has seen us at our worst and knows our darkest secrets and most depraved desires?

This moment God knows what you will face the rest of your life. Hear His promise: "In all things God works for the good of those who love Him, who have been called according to His purpose."[7]

Do not run in fear from our all-knowing God. There is no place to hide. Look to His love, grace, and mercy. Pray this prayer: "I'm ready! Search me, O God; show me my offensive ways. I believe you love, forgive and cleanse me. Draw me into a sweeter, more intimate fellowship with you." God will lift your load of sin and free your conscience. His omniscient power has eternal consequences. Draw on that power today!

1. Acts 15:16-18
2. Isaiah 65:24
3. Psalm 90:8
4. Psalm 139:2, 4
5. Ezekiel 11:5
6. Psalm 139:23-24
7. Romans 8:28

44

7

Beyond the Farthest Star
God's Omnipresence

Where can I go from your Spirit? Where can I flee from your presence? If I go up to the heavens, you are there; if I make my bed in the depths, you are there. If I rise on the wings of the dawn, if I settle on the far side of the sea, even there your hand will guide me...and the light become night around me, even the darkness will not be dark to you; the night will shine like the day, for darkness is as light to you.
Psalm 139:7-12

"Can anyone hide in secret places so I cannot see Him?" declares the Lord. "Do not I fill heaven and earth?" declares the Lord. Jeremiah 23:24

IN HIS BOOK, *One Holy Passion—The Attributes of God,* author R.C. Sproul relates this story about his freshman astronomy class: The professor's first question was, "Suppose we have a scale of one inch to one million miles. On that scale, how far do you think it would be to the nearest star— not including the sun—one-hundred, three-hundred, or five-hundred feet?"

Knowing the sun was about ninety-three million miles away, the students began mental calculations. Someone guessed one-hundred feet. Wrong. Five-hundred feet? Wrong again. The professor stated, "On a scale of an inch to one million miles, the nearest star would equal the distance from Pittsburgh to Chicago!"

He went on to explain that light, traveling at 186,000 miles per second, would encircle the earth seven-and-a-half times each second. The nearest star seen twinkling in the sky is four-and-a-half light years away—roughly twenty-four *trillion* miles!

Is it any wonder David wrote, "When I consider your heavens, the work of your fingers, the moon and the stars, which you have set in place, what is man that you are mindful of him, the son of man that you care for Him?"[1]

Do you feel insignificant compared with the universe? I hope so! Remember the distance of the nearest star, then stretch your mind to the farthest star and to stars yet undiscovered, then let me speak of God's omnipresence. Beyond the most distant galaxy, God is there in all His fullness. He is everywhere at once at all points in the universe. There is no place where God isn't.

So, is God big enough for you? The farthest star is right next to God and God is right next to you! Where can I go from your Spirit? Where can I flee your presence? There is no escaping God's presence.

GOD'S PRESENCE KNOWS NO LIMITS

God is everywhere; complete, infinite. Like His knowledge, wisdom, power, and authority, His presence knows no limits. God is close to everything; right next to everyone. If there were one square inch of the universe that God did not inhabit, He would not be omnipresent, but the Bible assures us: there is no place to hide from God.

Satan, the enemy of God and God's people, does not share that attribute. He is finite, limited in power and influence. He can be only in one place at a time. The book of Job states that Satan travels to and fro over the earth. God never travels. He is always everywhere present.

When Elijah and the prophets of Baal had their contest on Mt. Carmel to determine who is God, Baal did not answer by fire. Elijah taunted the sweaty prophets, "Shout louder...Surely he is a god! Perhaps he is deep in thought, or busy, or traveling. Maybe he is sleeping and must be awakened!"[2] Elijah's taunt was based on truth: only God can be equally present everywhere.

To sing, "Our God is an awesome God!" is a vast understatement, but it is the best we can do.

GOD'S OMNIPRESENCE MAKES THE UNIVERSE PERSONAL

We hear often about people who believe there is a god who created, but He just set the universe in motion, then backed off, like a child spinning a top who steps back to watch until it winds down. This view describes a mechanical, impersonal universe, but the Bible presents a universe that was created and is sustained and inhabited by a personal God.

God indwells all creation. A tree grows, taking up space. Does God's presence stop at the tree's bark? The concrete in a building or steel in an automobile—do they force God beyond their physical bounds? A golf ball dropped in a goldfish bowl displaces its volume in water, causing the water in the bowl to rise. A golf ball and water cannot co-exist in the same space. So does our presence on earth somehow displace God from the spot we occupy? No, God indwells *all* His creation, including us. If that were not so, we could conceive of an impersonal universe with God perhaps dwelling at our side, but not within.

However, the God presented in the Bible is intensely personal: "(He) is not far from each one of us. For in Him we live and move and have our being."[3] "In Him all things hold together."[4] "Through whom (Jesus) He made the universe. The Son is the radiance of God's glory and the exact representation of His being, sustaining all things by His powerful word."[5]

God's sustaining power gives new life to dormant grass each spring. Sap courses to tips of tree branches. Geese fly north, walleye migrate up river. All nature obeys the Creator's design and rests on His sustaining presence.

There is no Mother Nature, only Father Creator; God who permeates His creation and guides its structured rhythm in full harmony with His purposeful plan. The universe is personal because God is everywhere, all the time, keeping nature and history on course.

We think of Jonah trying to flee from the presence of God. How silly! But what Jonah attempted, we often attempt as we pray. Do we think we can conceal secret sins so God won't know about them? Do we complain that God is not near because He doesn't *feel* near? Our complaint reflects only feelings, not fact. God is always near.

We create emotional distance between ourselves and God in the same way we create distance in earthly relationships. Cutting off communication and refusing to be open will cool any relationship, even with God.

The truth of God's omnipresence should be our constant source of comfort in the midst of our sins, failings, and weaknesses. Even when we disappoint God and ourselves, He never leaves us, for He is omnipresent, always near, closer than near. God dwells within us!

So when troubling times come, don't try to run from God. There is no place to go where He will not be. When fear sweeps in, know that He understands. In the moment of deepest despair, embrace Him, and let His ever-present love enfold you.

1. Psalm 8:3
2. 1 Kings 18:27
3. Acts 17:27-28
4. Colossians 1:17
5. Hebrews 1:2-3

8

Holy! Holy! Holy!
God's Holiness

In the year that King Uzziah died, I saw the Lord seated on a throne, high and exalted, and the train of His robe filled the temple. Above Him were seraphs, each with six wings: With two they covered their faces.... "Woe to me!" I cried, "I am ruined! For I am a man of unclean lips...and my eyes have seen the King, the Lord Almighty." Isaiah 6:1-2, 5

Holy, holy, holy is the Lord God Almighty, who was, and is, and is to come. Revelation 4:8

OCCASIONALLY IN THE SCRIPTURES God parts the curtain that separates Heaven from Earth to give us a glimpse into the heavenlies. The passages listed above provide such a glimpse, allowing us to view a scene of worship.

Of the attributes of God already discussed—his sovereign, unchanging, self-existent, self-sufficient, all-powerful, all-knowing, everywhere-present being; and of the attributes yet to be examined—God's goodness, grace, mercy, love, and wrath; the attribute singled out in the worship scene portrayed in Isaiah 6 is *Holiness.*

We note in Isaiah's vision that the angels did not cry Love, Love, Love! or Grace, Grace, Grace! Not even Strength, Strength, Strength!. These are the attributes we talk about most often. The seraphs' ceaseless cry was, Holy! Holy! Holy! We must conclude, then, that there is something special about God's holiness.

Because God is the sum of perfection, and His attributes function in perfect balance, I do not claim that holiness is more important than other attributes, but it is clear that the Scriptures treat God's holiness as something special.

Holiness is God's beauty, glory and radiance. Holiness never ceases to be proclaimed day and night. Holiness is the sum of God's moral excellence. So pure and brilliant is God's holiness that mortals cannot behold it.

We understand Isaiah's terror: Woe is me! I am ruined! We understand because like us, Isaiah was contaminated by sin. But note that even the seraphs could not look on God's holiness. They used two of their six wings to cover their faces.

How awesome is God's holiness! Even angelic beings cannot look fully upon it. Like Moses shielded in a cleft of the rock as God passed by, we are fortunate to survive even a glimpse of God's full majesty.

Holiness is not a quality God has but something He is. Holiness pervades all His attributes. Holiness sums up God's moral excellence. His love is holy. God will never manipulate, deceive, or seek by love to compel anyone's allegiance. God's power, justice, and forgiveness are holy. Even God's wrath is holy wrath.

God's holiness insures that evil cannot touch Him. All His actions and words are pure, without false motives. The Spirit He sends to us is the Holy Spirit, who deals only in truth and purity for our good.

We can imagine something of God's love because we experience feelings of love. We can understand something of God's forgiveness because we give and receive forgiveness. But holiness? We have no personal experience to understand it. How easily we accept unholiness in our lives, looking upon it as natural and expected. We know sin well, but not holiness.

We create laws to protect ourselves from one another because we are unholy. Some say that Christians created the God of the Bible to be a crutch because they are emotionally weak. Why would a depraved people invent a God whose holiness only magnifies sin? Human nature always seeks to minimize its depravity, not shed bright light on it. We would invent God as a tired old man who would turn his head at humanity out of control and sigh, "Boys will be boys!"

In God's holy presence even angels cover their faces, and godly Isaiah cries out, Woe is me; I am ruined! God is and always has been holy, and His holy love provides a way for sinful people to draw near to live with Him eternally.

GOD'S HOLINESS DEFINES SIN

On a recent drive I spotted a police car parked just off the road, radar gun poised. How would the officer know who was speeding? He had a standard: thirty miles per hour. From that standard He could determine when a driver was violating the law.

Because God by nature is holy, He needs no standard beyond Himself. God's holiness defines sin. Isaiah's terror resulted from comparing Himself with that standard: "My eyes have seen the Lord."

Had Isaiah met another human, he would not have sensed his own uncleanness—we all compare our sins with the sins of others. We look at the black sins of a serial killer or child molester and our dark sins look medium gray. If we get a speeding ticket, though we know we deserve it, don't we feel that the policeman should be tracking down real criminals, not bothering citizens in a legitimate hurry?

We compare a light-gray speeding ticket with the deep black of drug dealers and rapists.

It is not our nature to accept perfection, purity and holiness as our standard for conduct. Many people are risking their eternal destiny on the presumption that the standard for entering into heaven is just above Adolph Hitler and Joseph Stalin.

The problem is, no man is the standard, God is. God's holiness places everyone on equal footing. "All have sinned and fall short of the glory of God."[1] That's why Billy Graham must seek forgiveness for himself as well as his hearers. By the standard of God's absolute holiness, there are no light-gray and dark-gray sins. Some sins may be less offensive to man and cause less harm than others, but compared with God's standard, all sin is black.

When we measure ourselves by someone morally inferior to ourselves, we may feel quite comfortable; but when we measure ourselves against God's holiness, we immediately feel the need for Jesus' cleansing power.

GOD SHARES HIS HOLINESS THROUGH JESUS

God's holiness casts us all as morally depraved, guilty sinners. If God were only holy and just, we would have no hope, but God is also love, full of compassion, grace and mercy. His grace protects us. God hid Moses in the cleft of the rock, allowing him to see only a fraction of the divine glory, for Moses could not survive the full radiance of God's presence. Later, when God descended to Mount Sinai to give Moses the Law, He warned Israel not to touch even the foot of the mountain lest they die.[2]

But God's love moved beyond mere protection. He was willing to share His holiness with mankind.

Picture this: You stand before Judge Jesus, the perfect image of the Father, pure and holy. The Judge passes sentence: Guilty! You know you are guilty, and you accept the sentence: death, eternal separation from God.

Then the judge takes off his robe and changes places with you. He who passed the death sentence takes the penalty on himself and dies in your place, thus releasing you from all guilt so you can be counted pure and holy, even though you are not. This is the love and generosity of God, who shares His holiness with us through Christ.

GOD'S GIFT OF HOLINESS CHANGES US

In addition to providing salvation, the most crucial experience of life, what will God's gift of holiness do for us? First, it will set us apart from the common, ordinary things of the world system.

God in His holiness lives above anyone or anything else, and so should we. The word *holy* in Scripture describes that which was set apart for God's special purpose. God commanded Moses, "Take off your sandals, for the place where you are standing is holy ground."[3] The ground where Moses stood before the burning bush—at that moment— was set aside for God's use, therefore it was holy. Temple objects and animals destined for sacrifice were called holy because they were set apart from common use for the service of God.

Christ's presence in our lives makes us holy in God's sight, and we are called to live above the ordinary. We seek higher values, think bigger thoughts, pray bigger prayers and expect the impossible; looking always to God for guidance. In Christ we become extraordinary people, citizens of God's kingdom on earth.

Second, God's holiness enables us to grow in personal holiness. The indwelling Holy Spirit creates a revulsion of sin. Sin loses its power over us. We see sin for what it truly is and we begin to react to sin as God does. What once seemed minor sin now brings conviction and distaste. God's holiness, shared with us through Jesus, changes us to become like Him.

53

God admonished Israel, "You are to be holy to me, because I, the Lord, am holy."[4] He did not say, "Be as holy as I am," for that would be impossible, but God called His people to a higher level of living, a nobler purpose in life.

God summons us to a life that reflects His holiness, and His call is not without the means of fulfillment. Let us devote ourselves solely to God and allow God's Spirit to change us into a holy people.

1. Romans 3:23
2. Exodus 19:13
3. Exodus 3:5
4. Leviticus 20:26

9

God Is Great and God Is Good
God's Goodness

As Jesus started on His way, a man ran up to Him and fell on his knees before Him. "Good teacher," he asked, "What must I do to inherit eternal life?" Why do you call me good?" Jesus answered, "No one is good—except God alone." Mark 10:17-18

AS I GREW UP, the Carlsons said a table grace that started, "God is great and God is good." The first qualities we learned about God as those words passed our lips were, God is great and good. In this reflection, we will consider God's eternal goodness.

"Enter His gates with thanksgiving and His courts with praise; give thanks to Him and praise His name. For the Lord is good and His love endures forever."[1] "You are good, and what you do is good."[2]

Good is a broad concept, a term we use loosely. At our house God was good; but the food we ate was good also. My pet turtle was a good turtle. Our house was a good house, our church was a good church. When we got one

55

foot of snow we said it was good we didn't get two feet of snow. When a snowfall canceled school, that was *very* good.

Because we use *good* so many ways, saying God is good lacks the drama we feel when we say God is holy or God is sovereign. But goodness is an essential part of God's being, not an acquired trait. God possesses eternal, never-changing goodness. He has never been more good than He is now, nor will He ever be less good.

Goodness is what motivates God to be kind, benevolent, full of good will, compassionate, understanding, and for-giving. His goodness is reflected in His desire to bless us and teach us how to live the abundant life, a life that brings pleasure to both Him and us. God's goodness causes Him to feel pleasure when we are satisfied and compassion when we are troubled.

 Because God is good, He always acts in goodness to-ward people. The fact that evil things happen does not result from some deficiency in God's goodness, but because mankind invited evil into the world and now must live with its consequences.

But even the presence of evil does not erode God's goodness. "And we know that in all things God works for the good of those who love Him."[3] Since God is good by nature, He always acts for the good of His people in every circumstance of life. Satan's nature, on the other hand, is the opposite. He never has your good in mind; goodness is not part of His nature.

OUR GOODNESS CANNOT MERIT SALVATION

Mark chapter ten tells about a rich young ruler who in-quired how he could be sure of gaining eternal life. He lived with today's most common spiritual delusion — more common than atheism, New Age, or the cults. It is the delusion that a person can be good enough for heaven.

Recognizing Jesus' goodness, the young ruler used an address found no where else in the Gospels: *Good Teacher.* Before answering the young man's question about eternal life, Jesus dealt with his concept of goodness. "Why do you call me good? No one is good—except God alone."[4] He dodged the respectful title, Good Teacher.

Wasn't Jesus good? Of course. Why, then, did He deflect "good" away from Himself to the Father? Jesus wanted to direct the conversation away from the delusion that anyone can keep God's commandments well enough to be considered good enough to merit heaven. A person who could be that good would not need a Savior. When Jesus pressed the young ruler to sell all he had, give it to the poor, and become His follower, he turned away. Bottom line: he wasn't good enough after all!

To understand salvation by grace, we must take this brief exchange between Jesus and the rich young ruler seriously. If Jesus, the sinless one, deferred "good" to God alone, salvation could never be by human effort. Good people, even the best people, cannot merit salvation, for God alone is the standard of goodness. Salvation has to be the gift of God's grace, because no one can measure up to God's standard.

If Jesus would not accept good as a title, don't place the hope for salvation in your goodness! "For it is by grace you have been saved, through faith—and this not from yourselves."[5] Personal goodness is not a factor in salvation.

EVERYONE EXPERIENCES GOD'S GOODNESS

Perhaps the best way to understand this is by looking at God's goodness expressed through the creation. After each creation day God saw that His work was good. The Bible declares God's general goodness: "He...sends rain on the righteous and the unrighteous."[6] You need not be a believer to experience His goodness. You can curse God, reject His church, ridicule His Word, and still experience God's goodness expressed through His creation.

Consider two farmers who live across the road from each other. One farmer begins the day blessing God, the other curses as he pulls on his work boots and coveralls. Both farmers plant crops. The machines of both occasionally break down. One farmer hums a hymn while he repairs a mower. The other curses God and Jesus repeatedly.

After their crops are planted, both wait for rain. Clouds form, thunder speaks softly, and the rain falls on the believer's fields but stops miraculously at the road, leaving the unbeliever's fields dry. Right? Wrong!

The rain falls on the just and the unjust. God's goodness allows both farmers to make a living and provide for their families because God is good.

The fragrance of a rose pleases the believer and unbeliever alike. The taste of a steak brings a smile to the believer and unbeliever. God's healing power built into the body fights off infection and broken bones heal for both believers and unbelievers. Both enjoy more healthy days than sick days, more strength than weakness, more happiness than sadness. Why? Because God is good.

Even in the face of unbelief, cursing, and ridicule, God allows people of all kinds to enjoy what He has created because He loves them and because He is good.

GOD IS THE SOURCE OF ALL GOODNESS

Are unbelievers capable of doing good? Yes. Can they brighten others' lives and lighten their load? Can they help in times of need? Of course. Though such acts of goodness cannot add up to salvation, all kind acts are good. The

Salvation Army food shelf feeds the hungry regardless of who donated the food, and that is good.

Goodness exists because God dwells in His world. The same principle governs our capacity to love. "We love because He first loved us."[7] God's love makes people capable of loving, believers and unbelievers alike. Goodness and kindness began with God, and the satisfaction people gain from doing good comes from God. The truth is, we can do good only because God is good.

GOD'S GOODNESS MAKES HIM APPROACHABLE

God's goodness is that part of His nature that moves Him to be full of good will toward all people. This settles a big question: How will God react toward me if I approach Him in my sinful state?

The Father will react exactly the way Jesus reacted toward sinners, for Jesus said, "Anyone who has seen me has seen the Father."[8] People came to Jesus with physical, emotional, and spiritual ailments and He was always kind. Like His Father, Jesus was good.

To be sure, there were times when Jesus sternly confronted the Pharisees, religious hypocrites of His day. They were phonies who played manipulative games with God and people. Jesus challenged them not because He lacked goodness, but because His goodness could not tolerate dishonesty in relationships.

Before the Prodigal Son received the robe of welcome back into his family, he made an honest confession: "Father I have sinned against heaven and against you; I am no longer worthy to be called your son."[9] The prodigal's restored relationship was built on honesty.

God's goodness may be the least praised of His attributes. Perhaps this is because His goodness is so close to us. Each day we live and move in His goodness, and as they say, "We can't see the forest for the trees." Yet my earliest prayer still rings true: God is great and God is good.

"Enter His gates with thanksgiving and His courts with praise; give thanks to Him and praise His name. For the Lord is good and His love endures forever; His faithfulness continues through all generations."[10]

1. Psalm 100:4-5
2 Psalm 119:68
3. Romans 8:28
4. Mark 10:18
5. Ephesians 2:8
6. Matthew 5:45
7. 1 John 4:19
8. John 14:9
9 Luke 15:21
10. Psalm 100:4

10

Amazing Grace
God's Grace

For the law was given through Moses; grace and truth came through Jesus Christ. John 1:17

For it is by grace you Have been saved, through faith—and this not from yourselves, it is the gift of God.

Ephesians 2:8

BEFORE I DEFINE GRACE, let me illustrate: One day your eight-year-old daughter is late coming Home from school, so late you notify the police. A search begins. Hours turn into sleepless days. Then they find her naked body in a nearby woods. The investigation turns up the killer—a teenage boy from a dysfunctional home, himself a victim of physical and sexual abuse.

You face several possibilities in dealing with your grief. As the killer is being transferred from jail to court, you could crash through the police guard and kill him. That would be vengeance. Or, you could watch while the courts convict him and sentence him to life in prison. That would be justice. Or you could visit the boy as he awaited trial, listen to his story, feel pity, and forgive him. That would be forgiveness. Or you could go to the judge, plead for the boy's pardon, welcome him into your home and adopt him; guide him as a son, naming him generously in your will. That would be grace.

With an enormous amount of strength from God, I can imagine forgiving the boy, but I can not even imagine extending grace. How fortunate for us that God does not think as we do! Each day He adopts into His family people who have cursed His name and abused His Son. He provides daily for His adopted children and gives them a full measure of His inheritance—for all eternity! That's grace.

We define grace as undeserved favor, with the focus on *undeserved*. If you feel you deserve God's favor based on what a nice person you are; that God can't help but smile on someone as adorable as you, then you have no idea of grace. Only when you recognize how totally unworthy you are will you fully appreciate grace.

The Bible links grace with forgiveness and salvation. "For it is by grace you have been saved through faith."[1] Eternal life is an undeserved gift, received only by grace through faith. Grace is the attribute of God through which salvation flows.

While God's goodness reaches believer and unbeliever alike, only believers enjoy grace. Recall the two thieves who were crucified with Jesus: One hurled insults at Jesus; the other acknowledged his guilt and pled for mercy. That thief received grace and the promise of paradise. The other did not. Though grace is available to all, only believers gain its benefits. Jesus is the only channel through which God's grace comes to us. "For the law was given through Moses; grace and truth came through Jesus Christ."[2]

There are four things we must know before we can fully understand God's grace:

MANKIND'S SINFUL STATE AND ALIENATION FROM GOD

Those who do not believe they are sinners will know grace only as a word from the Bible. Today's society shuns individual responsibility, often blaming failure on alleged diseases. Sin is merely a product of the social environment. The sinner cries, "It's not my fault!"

Those who reject accountability for sin sense no need for grace. The grace we experience in Christ does not rest on inherent positive qualities but on our guilt. Grace focuses on what we don't deserve, our unworthiness.

GOD'S JUSTICE

God's justice is what makes God's grace so gracious. Justice is getting what rebellion deserves—hell, an eternity of pain, hatred, and agony; total separation from God and His love. Hell would be justice, the penalty for violating God's holiness. Justice says we deserve hell.

But God is not only holy and just, He is also gracious, and grace sweeps us off our feet and brings tears of gratitude. If God were not the God of all grace, we would receive justice not salvation. Grace is beautiful because it is totally undeserved. Surely this should lead us to a life of humility and worship.

MANKIND'S SPIRITUAL IMPOTENCE

By ourselves, we cannot repair our broken relationship with God. Our first sin disqualified us from any claim to fellowship with Him, making us unholy. Kind words or generous gifts by unholy people do not patch things up with a holy God. Good works do not cancel out sin. Only the grace of Jesus can bring us into fellowship with the Father. Grace strikes down all self-righteousness.

GOD'S SOVEREIGN FREEDOM

God is free to give grace or withhold grace. He cannot be manipulated. He is beholden to no one. God could allow justice to give us what we deserve, and that would be fair; leaving no grounds for appeal. God owes us nothing but justice.

A French philosopher died muttering, "God will forgive me, that's His job." The philosopher was wrong. God does not *owe* forgiveness. He is free to give grace or withhold grace. That is what makes grace so remarkable.

God does not say, "I *must* give grace; my love compels me." Were that so, God would be a slave to His own love, which would force Him, contrary to His holy nature, to overlook sin. But God gives grace freely, not because of our merit, or even His love. He gives grace because He is gracious. Grace found a way to remove sin-guilt through Christ's death on the cross, fulfilling the claims of justice. God freely chooses to give grace each and every time, and that should speak to us.

Freely, freely, you have received;
Freely, freely, give.

ETERNAL, UNBOUNDED GRACE

Like God's other attributes, grace is eternal and unbounded. As much sin as there is in our world, God's grace is greater. God will never say, "My supply of grace has been used up! I have no more to give." But because grace is limitless, some people have concluded that it doesn't matter how they live—God's grace will avail. Can anyone deny having thought, when faced by temptation, "Oh well, God will forgive?"

And you were right! Out of the riches of His grace our Savior and Lord forgives our worst sins. That being so, why stop sinning? Paul dealt with that question: "What shall we say, then? Shall we go on sinning so that grace

64

may increase?"[3] God is lavish with His grace, and some think they can take advantage of Him without penalty, but consider this:

Suppose I decide to be unfaithful to my wife, start using alcohol and drugs, or run up huge debts I can't pay; will God forgive me? Yes. He forgives all sin. Then, if God forgives everything and anything, why not live in sin? If that thought has crossed your mind, search out Romans 6; ponder these issues:

Whose slave are you?
Willful, habitual sin—not just the occasional failure we all experience—will thrust you again into slavery to sin. Jesus will cease to be your master, fellowship with God will be broken. Sin will become the controlling force in your life, and you will find sin a bitter slave master.

God has something better for His children! "Sin shall not be your master, because you are not under law, but under grace."[4] Can a true child of God, knowing God's grace, deliberately choose to live in sin? Perhaps. But such a choice always brings consequences.

You reap what you sow.
"Do not be deceived: God cannot be mocked. A man reaps what he sows."[5] God in His grace forgives sin but He may not cancel sin's consequences. If I chose to practice the sins mentioned above, I would lose my position as a pastor, my marriage, and the respect of my family, friends, and congregation. Sin has consequences!

God will forgive alcohol abuse, but He may not heal a liver diseased by drink. God will forgive adultery, but He may not heal the marriage or a deadly disease that follows. God will forgive a murderer, but He may not spare the electric chair.

Christians may and do sin, and God forgives them; but sin *always* has consequences. It is never to anyone's advantage to disobey God. Never!

If these thoughts on God's grace have caused you to acknowledge your sin and the just punishment God could have required, you have made good progress. If you grasped the breadth and depth of God's grace so well that you thought perhaps you could exploit free grace to indulge in sin, congratulations! You are a prime candidate for grace, for you proved once again how depraved and utterly sinful is the human heart.

How indescribably great is the grace of God that He would save the likes of us. Amazing grace!

1. Ephesians 2:8
2. John 1:17
3. Romans 6:1
4. Romans 6:14
5. Galatians 6:7

11

Surely Goodness and Mercy
God's Mercy

The Lord is compassionate and gracious, slow to anger, abounding in love.... As a father has compassion on his children, so the Lord has compassion on those who fear Him. For He knows how we are formed, He remembers that we are dust. Psalm 103:8, 13-14

But because of His great love for us, God, who is rich in mercy, made us alive with Christ, even when we were dead in transgressions—it is by grace you have been saved.
                                        Ephesians 2:4-5

THE FIRST ATTRIBUTES OF GOD we discussed were big and grand, so far beyond our experience that they make us feel insignificant. God is sovereign, self-existing, self-sufficient, all powerful, all knowing, always present; so holy that even angels cover their eyes in His presence. These majestic qualities establish Him as God alone, with none to compare. We can scarcely imagine a being of such grandeur.

Then we discussed God's goodness and grace, attributes we can grasp in some measure for they strike close to home. Now we will consider *mercy,* the attribute, along with love, that connects us most personally with God.

Some Bible translators render the word for mercy as compassion—a good choice. Mercy is God's tenderheartedness, His loving care for hurting people.

When God met with Moses at the burning bush, He revealed not only His holiness, but His compassion. First God commanded, "Do not come any closer...Take off your sandals, for the place where you are standing is holy ground."[1] Then He said, "I have indeed seen the misery of my people in Egypt. I have heard them crying out because of their slave drivers, and I am concerned about their suffering."[2] God's mercy led Him to raise up Moses to lead Israel out of their misery.

Like all His attributes, God's mercy is eternal. He has never been more merciful or less merciful than He is today. Some, upon viewing God's severe judgments on the Children of Israel, have concluded that the Old Testament God was less merciful than the New Testament God, almost as though God had experienced a mid-life crisis between the Testaments and had mellowed out. Of course that is not so, for God has always been equally merciful.

It is true that the New Testament reveals God's grace more clearly than the Old Testament, which may lead to the view that His mercy had increased. Grace and mercy are so closely associated that they seem almost the same, but as we will discover, mercy and grace are complementary but not identical.

GRACE ADDRESSES SIN; MERCY ADDRESSES SIN'S MISERY

The previous discussion taught us that grace is the attribute through which we receive salvation: "By grace you have been saved through faith."[3] Grace addresses our standing before God as sinners. When justice decreed eternal punishment, grace accomplished full and undeserved forgiveness through Christ. Mercy, on the other hand, speaks to the misery sin brought into the world. God did not create a world filled with suffering. Adam and Eve enjoyed tranquility until their sin brought the curse that affected not only them and the Serpent, but the natural world as well.

Today our world is filled with death and misery in a thousand forms: the Oklahoma City bombing, North Dakota floods, the agony of cocaine babies. Everywhere we look misery abounds.

God's angels never experience grace or mercy for they know nothing of sin's guilt and misery. Angels do not need glasses at forty, or grow stiff and sore with arthritis, or die in drive-by shootings. Angels can only observe and wonder at the world mortals experience.

Though grace and mercy often appear together, this difference can be noted: Grace relates to the sin of individuals, while mercy touches to the whole world of misery. Thus grace and mercy minister both to the sin that condemns lost people to Hell, and to the consequences of sin that makes life on earth so miserable.

MERCY SERVES OUR SPIRITUAL NEEDS

Sin alienated mankind from God. He created Adam and Eve and gave them an open, enjoyable relationship with Himself, but when they sinned, they tried to hide, embarrassed by their nakedness. Fig leaf aprons provide a fitting metaphor for humanity's futile efforts to repair their broken relationship with God through self-effort.

From birth on we move away from obedience. We meet our first encounter with authority—parents—by disobeying. No one taught us to steal from the cookie jar. Mom said, "Don't take cookies without asking," and by nature we looked for the first opportunity to disobey. We call that original sin.

We treat God, the ultimate authority, the same way. We don't by nature hunger for an obedient walk with Him, but God's mercy meets our need by teaching the joy of obedience.

Mark tells how Jesus and the Twelve set out by boat to seek solitude, but upon reaching their destination they found a crowd waiting. "When Jesus landed and saw a large crowd, He had compassion (mercy) on them, because they were like sheep without a shepherd. So He began *teaching* them many things."[4] Mercy led to teaching.

Sin creates a miserable relationship with God which produces misunderstandings, distortions, doubt, guilt, fear, and religious legalism. God's mercy enlightens us, creating a spiritual hunger and repairing the broken relationship. Mercy draws us to God in reconciliation.

MERCY SUPPLIES OUR PHYSICAL NEEDS

Matthew's account of Jesus' search for solitude adds this: "When Jesus landed and saw a large crowd, He had compassion on them and *healed their sick*."[5] Jesus came to reveal what God was like, and though He did not heal every sick person He met, His many healings teach us that the Father cares about our aches and pains.

God created the world and mankind in perfection, and heaven will be free from the consequences of sin, but while we live on earth, we look to God's mercy to supply the health we enjoy. We have natural healing for our bodies, occasionally, miraculous healing. Mercy helps us cope with the misery we must live with day by day.

MERCY SUPPLIES OUR EMOTIONAL NEEDS

To illustrate justification by faith, we picture a court room where the Judge declares us innocent, though we know we are guilty. To illustrate God's power and majesty, we point to the vastness and grandeur of His universe. To picture the atonement, we visit the temple with the altar where the blood of a lamb is sprinkled. But how can we picture mercy, God's compassion for human misery?

We might portray God in a hospital emergency room or funeral home; or show Him at a lonely dinner table after a divorce or by a bedside, the pillow wet with tears upon learning of a spouse's unfaithfulness. We might see Him in a prison cell with an inmate filled with bitter regret or watching over the agony of a drug addict. God cares! When we hurt, He hurts. He cares for all kinds of pain.

Remember Star Wars? "May the Force be with you." The Force? A shallow allusion to an unknown power somewhat greater than us. To apply that term to the God of Abraham, Isaac and Jacob is a terrible insult.

A force has no feelings, and that cannot describe our God. He knows about feelings. His Son laughed at a wedding party, wept at a funeral, and cried out when the sin of the world fell on Him: "My God, my God, why have you forsaken me?"[6] Oh yes, God knows about feelings, and He cares.

Our capacity to love, think, laugh, feel sorrow, anger, peace, joy, and pain; these all came from the Source of all that exists when He created us in His image. God is Spirit, but not an unfeeling Spirit. Because He is full of mercy, there is nothing you feel that He does not feel. God's mercy heals our emotional hurts as well as our spiritual and physical hurts. Do not think for a moment that your pain does not have God's full attention. He is always present, always aware of needs, and always full of mercy.

71

The promise of Psalm 23 belongs to us today. "Surely goodness and mercy will follow me all the days of my life, and I will dwell in the house of the Lord forever."[7]

1. Exodus 3:5
2. Exodus 3:7
3. Ephesians 2:8
4. Mark 6:34
5. Matthew 14:14
6. Matthew 27:46
7. Psalm 23:6 KJV

12

Love Divine, All Loves Excelling

God's Love

This is how God showed His love among us: He sent His one and only Son into the world that we might live through Him. I John 4:9

THOUGH THE ENGLISH LANGUAGE IS WARM and rich, when it comes to the word *love*, we are cold and impoverished. We say, I love seafood! To our spouses we say, I love you. We say, God is love. In our tongue, love is love. However, New Testament Greek had several words for the various affections we describe as love.

Phileo spoke of love between friends, as in Philadelphia, the city of brotherly love. *Eros* (though not used in the Bible) referred to romantic love, as in erotic. *Agape* was the word New Testament writers used for God's love, a deep, pure, unconditional, eternal love. Agape love will be our focus in this discussion.

LOVE IS BUT ONE OF GOD'S MANY ATTRIBUTES

Because love is the most commonly discussed of God's attributes—among believers and unbelievers alike—there is a tendency to reduce God to that single attribute. This is a common view outside the church, but you also find it among church people who have limited understanding of the Bible and of God's true nature.

We hear people say, "God is love. He would never send anyone to hell!" They assume that love is God's only attribute and that love controls all He does. A God of love would not press for justice or punish evil.

If that were true, God would be less caring than we humans. Is there a parent who hasn't disciplined a child out of love? When your child disobeys, you discipline, because you care and you know that the discipline is in your child's best interest. You discipline because you love.

Some people seem to consider God incapable of doing what parents do daily, which would make God's love less than humanity's, but "The Lord disciplines those He loves."[1] He disciplines out of a holy love based on justice.

Not to discipline would be neglect. God is love, but He is more than mere sentiment. All of His attributes function in perfect harmony. But having said that, we should note that God's love is not without warmth.

GOD'S LOVE IS WARM AND EMOTIONAL

God's love is personal, warm, emotional. God's love feels good; it heals, drives out fear, provides security, a sense of safety. We rest in God's love. But it has grown popular in our society to acknowledge that life has a spiritual dimension without admitting there is a God. God is thought of as energy.

May the Force be with you. How cold and empty! Let's say you have sinned and you feel terrible. Or you make a huge mistake that hurts many people and you can't forgive yourself, much less feel good about yourself. Or perhaps your spouse says, "I don't love you anymore." At such times, would you prefer a Force or a loving God who understands and cares?

The next time someone mentions cosmic energy, proudly tell them about the God of Abraham, Isaac and Jacob. Tell them about Jesus.

GOD'S LOVE CANNOT BE COERCED

Without doubt we are the objects of God's love, but saying that brings both comfort and danger. We might conclude that something about us compels God to love us, and that would be dangerous.

Indeed God loves us, but not because we won His heart. No one is so adorable that God can't help but love him or her. We struggle with this concept because in our experience we see something in another person that awakens a love response in us. It could be personality, generosity, compassion, or interest in us. Whatever it is, we sense the stirring of an emotional response that may grow until one day we say, "I love you!"

We must not assume that something in us prompts God to love us. God loves because it is His nature to love, whether we are lovable or unlovable. "God demonstrates His own love for us in this: While we were still sinners, Christ died for us."[2]

God loves us in our worst rebellion because His love does not depend either on any worth in us or in our willingness to return His love. God can command us to love our enemies because He loves His enemies.

75

No worthiness inherent in us attracts God's love, still we have great worth in God's eyes because He loves us. To say, "I have worth, therefore God loves me," places me in the center. Pride mounts and we begin to think, "God must see something He can't resist!"

That was a danger the Children of Israel faced when God was about to lead them into the Promised Land and re-establish His covenant with them. He took steps to insure against false pride. First, God made a statement that was sure to stir the ego: "For you are a people holy to the Lord your God. The Lord your God has chosen you out of all the peoples on the face of the earth to be His people, His treasured possession."[3]

Treasured possession! A feel-good statement, for sure. But about the time the Israelites were concluding that God had made a brilliant choice, He humbled them: "The Lord did not set His affection on you and choose you because you were more numerous than other people, for you were the fewest of all peoples. But it was because the Lord loved you."[4]

No merit in anyone coerces God's love. God chooses to love me, and He loves me immensely, not because of what I am but because it is His nature to love.

GOD'S LOVE IS ETERNAL

When I say God's love is eternal, you may think, "Yes, God will always love me," but hear God's words to Israel: "I have loved you with an *everlasting* love; I have drawn you with loving kindness."[5] Everlasting means without beginning or end. God loved us from eternity. He loved us before we were born! "He chose us in Him before the creation of the world."[6]

God was aware of you prior to your birth. Back then He set His love upon you, and His love is as vast as eternity. He loves you even though He has already seen your worst moment. How can God love like that? Because He does not depend on you for a reason to love.

"Who shall separate us from the love of Christ. Shall trouble or hardship or persecution or famine or nakedness or danger or sword...?"[7] No matter what you have done or will do, God's love will not cease. Nothing can separate you from God's love because He does not depend on your loveability.

The trials listed above can disrupt love between people, for our love depends on the other person's response. We love the lovable, but we struggle to love our enemies. To do that, we must discover God's love, a love that does not rest on some goodness in the other person to stir that love.

GOD'S LOVE IS ALWAYS SELFLESS

What if no one had ever responded to God's love; not one soul believed, obeyed, or loved Him? What if everyone ever born had cursed God to His face? Would "God is Love" still stand as truth? Of course. It is staggering to think that God loves sinners like us, yet it is true. God never loves for His benefit; always for our benefit. If not one person responded, God would still love.

God's love is never wasted because it does not depend on a response. God loves the most hardened, vile person as much as He loves Billy Graham, you and me. God loves even though He may receive only evil in return. God is love, and He is always true to His nature.

A teenager may compromise virtue in order to gain acceptance, sacrificing personal standards for what he or she perceives to be love. How many times we hear, "But we love each other!" Compromising love is always self-centered, expecting something in return.

God never loves on that basis. He does not demand love in return, hence He does not need to bargain for our love. God's love is uniquely different from human love.

Love can be measured by how much it is willing to give. Did Jesus die on the cross in a desperate attempt to win human allegiance? Did the Father give His Son to earn gratitude? Jesus did not die to compel us to love the Father, he died to demonstrate the Father's love. If not one soul responded to the cross, God would not become less loving, for as we noted in Romans 5:8, "God demonstrates His love for us in this: While we were still sinners, Christ died for us."[7] The cross showed how much God's love is willing to give.

You can curse God's name and still He will love you; or you can bow in gratitude and worship, but neither cursing nor bowing affects God's love. He loves for our benefit, never His. Accept that love and the incredible offer it includes—fellowship with God!

1. Hebrews 12:6
2. Romans 5:8
3. Deuteronomy 7:5-6
4. Deuteronomy 7:7-8
5. Jeremiah 31:3
6. Ephesians 1:4
7. Romans 8:35

13

What Makes God Angry?
God's Wrath

I lift my hand to heaven and declare: As surely as I live forever...I will take vengeance on my adversaries and repay those who hate me. Deuteronomy 32:40-41

THE STORY IS TOLD of a rabbi and a student he had been teaching for some time:

"Do you feel that you know me?" asked the rabbi.

"Yes, Rabbi," replied the student.

"Do you know what makes me angry?"

"No, Rabbi, I do not."

"Then you do not yet know me."

Suppose our reflections on God's attributes ended and I had not mentioned God's wrath, and one day the Lord confronted you: "As you have listened to Pastor Len describing me and my attributes, do you feel you know me?"

"Yes Lord," you would say, "I feel I know you better than before".

"Did Pastor Len tell you what makes me angry?"

"No, Lord, he didn't."

"Then you do not yet know me!"

When God's wrath comes up, why do we automatically feel the need to apologize, as though God had a character flaw? God certainly isn't embarrassed to tell us about that part of His nature, nor should we be embarrassed, but often we are. Consider the following scenarios:

It is Thursday. You know that this Sunday your pastor will preach on God's wrath. The following Sunday he will preach on God's faithfulness. The phone rings. A person you just met says, "As you know, we are new in town. We're looking for a church home and we heard about your church. Would you suggest we visit this Sunday or next?" Why would you be tempted to say, "Next Sunday, please!"

Or, it's Sunday morning. You arrive at church and note the sermon topic: "The Wrath of God." Do you check for the nearest exit? Or bite your tongue to make your eyes water so you can say, "Honey, I think I'm coming down with something. Can we go home?"

It might surprise you to know that the Bible refers more often to God's wrath against wickedness than it does to His love and compassion. If God does not hesitate to make His wrath known, would I not do both Him and you a disservice if I failed to declare that part of who He is, or if I spoke apologetically as if to say, "Don't hold that against Him!"

If you really want to know God, you must learn what makes Him angry.

Technically, God's wrath is not an attribute. The attributes that lead to wrath are holiness and justice. Since by nature God is just and holy, wickedness in all its forms must repel Him. "The wrath of God is being revealed from heaven against all the godlessness and wickedness of men who suppress the truth by their wickedness."[1]

God hates sin because He is holy. He must punish sinners because He is just. Punishment is God's wrath.

GOD'S WRATH WILL BE JUST AND FAIR

Possibly the idea of God's wrath makes us uncomfortable because on a human level wrath implies loss of self-control. When you incur someone's wrath, that person will more than likely go out-of-control. We use terms like burning up, seeing red, irrational, in a rage. Though this is common among people, we must not transfer such expressions to God. His wrath is severe but never arbitrary, never out of control, always just; no less or more than is deserved.

But if wrath is considered a character flaw in humans, why not in God? Would not God still be God if He didn't know wrath? Rather than being a divine character flaw, we will see wrath as the opposite. Without wrath, God—who hates sin—would be helpless to do anything about it. Though grieved by blasphemy, He would be powerless to defend His name.

God's wrath is never capricious or arbitrary. It is as necessary to His perfection as are love and mercy. His attributes function in perfect harmony. For example, I am deeply opposed to the Colombian drug cartel, but I am powerless to do anything about it. Would you want God to be like me?

Our hope rests on justice, the knowledge that one day righteousness will triumph and evil will be punished fairly and justly. That hope finds fulfillment in the wrath of God.

Let us imagine that all my children come home for Christmas. While I leave the house to buy a gallon of milk, a gunman enters and brutally murders my family. He is caught and tried, but goes free on a technicality. Where is my hope for justice if there is no wrath of God? I would live with despair.

Let us say the killer continues his life of crime and one day dies in a blaze of gunfire with the police, cursing God and man as he dies. I have full confidence that justice will be served—if not here, then there, in eternity. If God was powerless to judge evil, there would be no *there*. (heaven) judn

God's wrath, then, is part of His perfection. Sin must be punished, for to ignore sin would be to deny holiness, justice, and omnipotence. In the struggle of good against evil, God will have the last word. Sin will be punished and righteousness will be rewarded.

GOD'S WRATH LIES BEYOND HUMAN MISERY

Sin can be expressed through a variety of actions, behaviors and thoughts, but the ultimate sin, that which brings a person under the wrath of God, is unbelief, the rejection of God's plan of salvation in Jesus. A person's response to Jesus determines heaven or hell.

The thief on the cross at Calvary would go one of two directions when he died. For one, destiny would not be determined by his thievery but by his response to Jesus. He believed Jesus' claim to be the Savior and gained a place in Paradise. That must be the way for us, too.

Rejecting Jesus makes us the object of God's wrath because we are all sinners, "by nature objects of wrath."[2] We share the sinful human nature that rejects divine authority and chooses disobedience. God's wrath leads to Hell, the only alternative to Heaven.

We hear people say, "I couldn't possibly go to Hell, I've already been there." We may suffer trauma, war, natural disasters, painful, debilitating illnesses; could Hell be worse? Sadly, the Bible reveals that God's wrath against sin will bring agony beyond any human misery.

Though the Scriptures describe Hell in a variety of ways, none comes close to Hell's reality. *Gehenna,* one New Testament word translated Hell, referred to the Valley of Hinnom just to the west of Jerusalem where the city's

82

rubbish was burned. It was a smelly, filthy, depository of everything worthless, whose smoke and flames provided the imagery for Hell.

Hell is a place of despair, not for a time, but for eternity. "Where their worm does not die and the fire is not quenched."[3] Hell is a place with no rest, no moment of relief; not for a time but for eternity. Hell is outer darkness—the total absence of light, the loss of everything good, pleasurable and fair. Hell can offer no friendship because love is absent. Light and love reside only in God, and the essence of Hell is separation from God.

In Hell there is no peace, only confusion, hatred, lies, and deceit; no fairness, nothing worth living for. Hell is a place of remorse, gnashing of teeth—you will hate yourself. You will exist eternally knowing you rejected Christ and there is no second chance. You will want to die, but you can't.

GOD HAS PROVIDED DELIVERANCE FROM WRATH

God freely chose to provide a means to escape the fearful consequences of sin. He sent His Son, Jesus Christ, who willingly took our guilt and penalty upon Himself on the cross. All the sinner needs to do to escape God's wrath is to believe in Jesus, to accept the gift of salvation Jesus purchased by His blood.

Unbelief—the rejection of Jesus—places us under God's wrath. If that were not so, from what would we be saved? If there is no accountability to God, no punishment for sin (as some claim), why would anyone need Jesus? .

What if God had administered His wrath the moment we rebelled? He would have been entirely justified in doing so. Then the opportunity to find forgiveness in Christ would be lost. But He delayed His wrath. "God's kindness leads you toward repentance."[4]

Some understand God's patient love and thank Him, others interpret the delay in judgment as evidence of weakness, or an inability to do anything about evil. Some conclude that God's wrath doesn't exist.

Consider Sodom and Gomorrah. The remarkable thing is not that God destroyed two cities for their wickedness, the remarkable thing is that God waited so long. He allowed Abraham plea after plea for the cities' survival. Abraham asked God to spare the city if he could find fifty righteous people, then forty-five, then forty and all the way down to ten. Each time God agreed. But ten righteous people could not be found.

How do you perceive God's response? Over-reacting, out of control, wild-eyed? The glory of God is in His patience, and controlled wrath magnifies that patience. God's kindness leads us to repentance.

One day God's wrath will come. His holy character demands it. But "Jesus...rescues us from the coming wrath."[5] Delayed judgment provides opportunity for rescue. Be reconciled to God through Jesus today. Acknowledge your sin, ask forgiveness, give your life to Jesus. Once you have done that, you have nothing to fear, for you will no longer be an object of wrath but a child in God's family. Jesus bore your punishment on the cross, He paid the penalty. You are free!

1. Romans 1:18
2. Ephesians 2:3
3. Mark 9:48
4. Romans 2:4
5. 1 Thessalonians 1:10

14

Great Is Thy Faithfulness

God's Faithfulness

Know therefore that the Lord your God is God; He is the faithful God, keeping His covenant of love to a thousand generations of those who love Him and keep His commandments. Deuteronomy 7:9

Here is a trustworthy saying: If we died with Him, we will also live with Him; if we endure, we will also reign with Him; If we disown Him, He will also disown us; if we are faithless, He will remain faithful, for He cannot disown Himself. 2 Timothy 2:11-13

ONE OF MY FIRST EXPERIENCES on jury duty was to listen to a case in which two men had a verbal agreement concerning a business deal. The law provides that verbal agreements are binding without documents and signatures, providing it can be proved that both parties understood the same thing when making the agreement.

If you have ever served on a jury, you will be amazed how people can swear to tell the whole truth, then lie and distort facts. Their actions are not consistent with their vows—they are not faithful.

An athlete signs a contract to play for a certain amount of money for so many years. Then he has one or two good years and he insists on more pay or he won't play. That might balance out if, after one or two bad years, the athlete agreed to reduced pay; but that happens only in a team owner's dreams. Some athletes are not faithful.

Fewer than half of the couples who pledge faithfulness in marriage fulfill that pledge. The growing practice of pre-nuptial agreements reveals the deterioration of integrity in wedding vows. The pre-nuptial agreement says, "I don't plan to take this commitment seriously enough to risk losing half of my financial holdings. Sign here—black ink for easy copying." Some couples don't intend to be faithful.

Unfaithfulness to a promise may result from unforeseen circumstances: "I'm sorry, I can't pay these bills. Our family had catastrophic medical problems and I am bankrupt." But most of the time, unfaithfulness results from a simple lack of integrity. People of high moral character will do what they pledge.

Faithfulness has never been a problem for God. He always has been and always will be faithful. God's character and perfection make it impossible for God to be less than faithful. What He says He will do.

WE DEPEND ON GOD'S FAITHFULNESS TO HIS WORD

We believe in heaven though we have never been there. We believe Jesus lived, died, rose from the grave and now sits at the right hand of the Father, yet we have never met Jesus in person. We believe in God the Father, creator of heaven and earth though we have never seen Him. We believe in the reality of sin though sin has no physical properties. We believe that the blood of Christ will wash away sin though you can't see that happen.

We believe these things because God said they were true and we have utter faith that God's Word is reliable. We believe because its impossible for God to lie.

Morning and evening, summer, fall, winter and spring, we depend on God to honor His promise. When Noah left the ark after the flood, God said, "As long as the earth endures, seed time and harvest, cold and heat, summer and winter, day and night will never cease."[1] Why did the sun rise this morning and the trees, grass and plants survive the cold of winter? Because of Mother Nature? No; God our Father said these things would happen. We can count on God to do what He says.

God faithfully tells us the worst news as well as the best. The worst news is, "The wages of sin is death." But the same verse also gives us the best news: "The gift of God is eternal life in Christ Jesus our Lord."[2]

Every time you talk about what God will do for you, you are exercising faith in His faithfulness. Every time you pray you exercise faith that God is really listening as He said He would. You share your faith with a non-believer because you believe that people without Christ are eternally lost, as God said they were. Our every act as Christians rests on confidence that God will be faithful to His word.

GOD'S PROMISES ARE RELIABLE, HIS TIMING PURPOSEFUL

"With the Lord a day is like a thousand years, and a thousand years are like a day. The Lord is not slow in keeping His promise, as some understand slowness."[3] You don't have to be a believer very long to learn that God's timing and our timing are not the same. Occasionally they coincide and we get all excited and conclude that we have some control over God. But it won't be long until we meet up with the reality: "With the Lord a day is like a thousand years, and a thousand years are like a day."[3]

God told Abraham that Sarah would have a son, though she was barren and old. The promise, given when Abraham was seventy-five, was not fulfilled until he was he was ninety-nine! Twenty-four years of waiting and wondering if God would be faithful. God is always faithful to His word.

God told Isaiah that a virgin would conceive and bear a son who would be called Emmanuel, God with us. At just the right time, the promise was fulfilled: "When the time had fully come, God sent His Son born of a woman."[4] Seven-hundred years has passed since Isaiah wrote God's promise. God's word is always reliable, His timing purposeful.

Nearly two thousand years ago Jesus said, "Yes, I am coming soon."[5] Has He forgotten His word? We should not grow impatient, for if a thousand years is as a day, figuratively, only two days have passed. Will Jesus come again? Of course. He is faithful to do what He says.

When God says He disciplines those He loves, He will discipline. When God promises He will not allow believers to be tempted beyond their strength without providing a way of escape, you can count on it. His strength is made perfect through weakness; you will reap what you sow; the gates of hell will not prevail against the church—all God's promises are reliable.

When God says you can personally know the power that brought about Jesus' resurrection, you can be certain that power is available; when, where, and in what form rests entirely with God, but you can be sure He will be faithful to His word, and at just the right time.

GOD IS FAITHFUL TO HIMSELF

God is without beginning or end—eternal. All His attributes have always existed in the form and power they now exist. God was faithful to His own person before the universe came to be, before He created mankind to be the object of His faithfulness.

Have you been disappointed in yourself? God never has. He Has never broken a promise or said one thing and done another. He has never changed His mind or been embarrassed by a memory. Through eternity, God has been faithful to Himself. He could not act out of character—lie, cheat, steal, or tempt someone with evil. God is faithful to His holiness. He could not possibly be less than He is this moment.

Remember that all of God's attributes function fully and simultaneously in perfect balance. No attribute ever contradicts or conflicts with another. God is love and He loves faithfully. He is all-powerful and faithfully exercises His power, guided by perfect wisdom. Since He is all-knowing, God administers justice perfectly. Because He is just, punishment and reward will be balanced perfectly. God must judge sin because He is holy, but because He is also love, God provides grace so that unholy beings can enjoy fellowship with Him through Christ.

To know and understand God, we must view His attributes as a complete package, each attribute in full harmony with the others. Some picture God so filled with wrath that His love can't be felt. Or God so filled with love that He can neither judge evil or defend His name. Stressing one attribute to the neglect of another distorts our concept of God and often leads to heresy.

God is the sum of all His attributes, the very definition of perfection. This harmony of attributes is the ribbon that binds together our vision of God, revealing to wondering mankind what He is like.

1. Genesis 8:22
2. Romans 6:23
3. 2 Peter 3:8
4. Galatians 4:4
5. Revelation 22:20

Editors' Note: *Mother's Day arrived as Pastor Len was draw-ing his sermons on the attributes of God to a close. He paused in the series to recognize the special day. We found his thoughts so refreshing; we felt they belonged on these pages.*

15

The Mother Side of Father God

As a mother comforts her child, so will I comfort you; and you will be comforted over Jerusalem. When you see this, your heart will rejoice.   Isaiah 66:13-14

THIS MOTHER'S DAY THEME provides a fitting con-clusion to our reflections on the attributes of God. What is God like? Is He essentially male? Though God chose to make Himself known in Scripture as the Heavenly Father, the fact is, "God is spirit,"[1] and spirit is without gender.

You can view this truth in two ways: God is neither male nor female; or, God is both male and female. I prefer the latter, because the characteristics we identify as mascu-line and feminine all originated in the Creator.

"So God created (mankind) in His own image, in the image of God He created him; male and female He created them."[2] Where did femininity come from? It could have come only from the Creator. Femininity reflects the divine image every bit as much as masculinity. Only together can either male or female perfectly reflect God's image.

Many in today's society seek to blur the differences between the sexes. Female rock singers shave their heads or wear masculine hair styles and clothes. *Androgynous*—they call it—having the characteristics or nature of both male and female. The gender of some fashion models is not easily distinguished at first glance.

I surely don't object to women in business or industry dressing comfortably, but must they wear power suit and tie and talk about the Green Bay Packers' latest draft pick?

The biblical perspective of women, that which makes them feminine, includes far more than fashion. We should highlight, not obscure, this perspective. Femininity is as much a part of God's nature as is masculinity, and women reflect God's image in ways men cannot. We should celebrate the uniqueness of male and female. Together they reflect the image of God.

Of course men and women differ. Men tend to talk about facts and stuff. Women talk about feelings and relationships. God is just as concerned about feelings and relationships as He is about facts and stuff. Men tend to be independent, while women tend towards interdependence. Men often prefer to go it alone, often refusing help. Women tend to invite others into their lives. Doesn't the Trinity model interdependence? Men bond by accomplishing tasks together. Women bond by talking, sharing life experiences. Doesn't God talk to us and share Himself with us?

The bottom line is this: God is the highest, most perfect expression of what is masculine, and the highest, most perfect expression of what is feminine.

Whatever makes a women feminine—from her body to her hormones to her way of thinking and feeling—all comes from God the Father. The gender tension arose partly because God chose to be called Father, which led some to conclude that He is essentially masculine. But if God created mankind, male and female, in His image, He *must* be both. It cannot be otherwise.

However, calling God *Father* may lack a positive ring in these days of rising feminism, failing dads, and social trauma. We properly lay many of today's family problems at the feet of fathers who have abandoned their responsibility. When a youngster asks, "What is God like?" we realize the answer we gave with confidence fifty years ago won't do. How can you tell the child of an absent or abusive dad, "God is like your father"?

For such a child we must ask, "Who loves you and is always there for you?" The child may reply, "my mother, or stepmother," perhaps a grandmother or an aunt; perhaps a social worker or teacher. To that child we must answer, "God is like her; the person who loves you." God would like that answer, for He created women to reflect His image.

Luke 15 includes three parables—stories—Jesus told to illustrate how important each person is to God. The stories show that God will search tirelessly for His own and wait patiently for the straying to return, even while they sow wild oats. Two of the stories present male images, the third, a female image.

The first story likens God to a shepherd who has ninety-nine sheep in the sheepfold, but who leaves them unprotected to search for one lost sheep. The second story pictures God as a father whose son leaves home, squanders his inheritance, then realizing his error, repents. The son returns home and finds the father waiting with open arms.

The third story pictures God as a woman. She has ten valuable coins, but loses one. She searches frantically throughout her house until she finds it. The parable presents God as a responsible, caring woman searching tirelessly for what is hers. Jesus did not hesitate to picture God as a woman, for women reflect the divine image as truly as men.

FATHER GOD GAVE BIRTH TO ALL LIFE AND CREATION

When Hallmark set up a card shop in a far corner of Eden, there was no Mother's Day section. Adam and Eve are the only people in history who could never honor a mother. They received life through creation. We could say that the Father gave birth to Adam and Eve.

Like earthly parents, the Father brought them into the world bearing His image; He shared with them the life that was Himself. Since creation, the honor of life-giving has rested with women, often with great inconvenience, always with pain. Mothers trace their life-giving role to Eden, to Eve and Adam and to Creator God. Giving birth and life is a feminine image of Father God.

All life forms—human, animal, vegetable—came from the womb of creation. Perhaps that is why the entry of sin affected nature as well as mankind. "Cursed is the ground because of you...it will produce thorns and thistles for you."[3] The curse subjected humans to weakness, death, and decay, and turned the pristine garden into a thistle field.

God's new creation will redeem both mankind and nature: "The whole creation has been groaning as in the pains of childbirth right up to the present time. Not only so, but we ourselves...groan inwardly as we wait eagerly for our adoption as sons, the redemption of our bodies."[4]

The sufferings of nature are pictured as labor pains, a strictly feminine image. Matthew 24 lists signs Jesus said would accompany the end of the age: wars, rumors of wars, famines, earthquakes. "All these are the beginning of the birth pains."[5] Again, the feminine image. The Scriptures cast God's work at the beginning and end of the age in the image of motherhood.

FATHER GOD GIVES SPIRITUAL BIRTH AND NURTURE

Jesus' familiar words to Nicodemus present the clearest analogy of God's motherhood. Jesus tells His late-night visitor, "I tell you the truth, no one can see the kingdom of God unless he is born again."[6] Spiritual life begins with a new birth, with God's Spirit as the life-giving agent. The imagery is motherhood, feminine.

Paul tells the Ephesian Christians, "God who is rich in mercy, made us alive with Christ even when we were dead in transgressions."[7] Made alive, born anew, born of the Spirit, born of God—favorite expressions of John and Paul. The Heavenly Father manifests His mother side each time a soul is born again.

For the most part, mothers guide their children from infancy into adult years. While fathers help, the big part of the task falls to mothers. In our spiritual lives, God oversees the maturing process. He guides through the example of Christians, through experience, prayer, Bible study, and worship. Just as mothers give us physical life and guide us as we mature, so God "mothers" us spiritually. Isaiah 66 pictures God as a mother who nurses Her baby, carries it, bounces it on Her knee, and comforts it.

God promises the same kind of care and nurture for His people today.

FATHER GOD AND MOTHER LOVE

When we search for a model of the purest, most enduring love on earth, we turn to mother love. A bond grows between mother and child that can never exist between a father and child. A unique closeness develops during pregnancy, birth and the nurturing process that follows.

Mother's intuition senses things going on in a child that even the best of fathers can't know.

Most often Mother makes the home secure, warm, and accepting. A mother wants the best for her child, which is why a sweaty, three-hundred-pound athlete with no front teeth will smile into the TV camera and say, "Hi, Mom!"

When the Israelites felt forsaken and utterly on their own, God spoke words they could not fail to understand: "Can a mother forget the baby at her breast and have no compassion on the child she has borne? Though she may forget, I will not forget you!"[8] God spoke gently to His people as a mother, not as a father.

What is the source of mother love? All that we are, our feelings, thoughts, and capabilities, come from God. The distinctive love we call mother love reflects our Father God. He is not the least embarrassed to be identified with motherhood.

We will continue to call God Father, for that is how He identified Himself in Scripture, and that is how Jesus addressed Him. Does that suggest that God is primarily masculine as opposed to feminine? Not in the least! The riches of femininity express the image of God, as do good human qualities, male or female. We rejoice and give thanks for the mother side of God our Father.

1. John 4:24
2. Genesis 1:27
3. Genesis 3:17-18
4. Romans 8:22-23
5. Matthew 24:8
6. John 3:3
7. Ephesians 2:4-5
8. Isaiah 49:15

Pass the blessing on!

Let us know your thoughts if you have been blessed by reading "What Is God Like?"

Thank you.

River City Press
Publishing Life-changing Books

4301 Emerson Avenue North
Minneapolis, MN 55412
1-888-234-3559

www.rivercitypress.net
publisher@rivercitypress.net